First World War
and Army of Occupation
War Diary
France, Belgium and Germany

60 DIVISION
Divisional Troops
60 Sanitary Division
29 February 1916 - 30 November 1916

WO95/3029/6

The Naval & Military Press Ltd
www.nmarchive.com
Published in association with The National Archives

Published by

The Naval & Military Press Ltd

Unit 10 Ridgewood Industrial Park,

Uckfield, East Sussex,

TN22 5QE England

Tel: +44 (0) 1825 749494

www.naval-military-press.com

www.nmarchive.com

This diary has been reprinted in facsimile from the original. Any imperfections are inevitably reproduced and the quality may fall short of modern type and cartographic standards.

© Crown Copyright
Images reproduced by permission of The National Archives, London, England, 2015.

Contents

Document type	Place/Title	Date From	Date To
Heading	WO95/3029/5		
Heading	60th Division Sanitary Section 1916 Feb-1916 Nov		
Heading	War Diary of Sanitary Section 60th (London) Divn. From 29th Febry 1916 To (Volume 1)		
War Diary	Sutton Veny	29/02/1916	21/06/1916
Miscellaneous	Nominal Roll of Sanitary Section No. Officer in Command, Lieut. H.S. Tebbitt		
Heading	Sanitary Section 60th (London) Division Appendix B (3 Sheets) 3/3/16 War Diary		
Miscellaneous	Sanitary Section-60th London Division	03/03/1916	03/03/1916
Miscellaneous	Instructions for Sanitary Inspection	03/03/1916	03/03/1916
Miscellaneous	Appendix "C" Of 1st May 1916		
Heading	War Diary of Sanitary Section 60th Division B.E.F. From 24th June 1916 To 31st July 1916 (Sheets)		
War Diary	Sutton Veny	24/06/1916	24/06/1916
War Diary	Southampton	24/06/1916	24/06/1916
War Diary	Le Havre	25/06/1916	26/06/1916
War Diary	Abbeville	26/06/1916	26/06/1916
War Diary	Petit Houvin	27/06/1916	27/06/1916
War Diary	Le Flers	28/06/1916	28/06/1916
War Diary	Villers Chatel	29/06/1916	14/07/1916
War Diary	Hermaville	15/07/1916	31/07/1916
Heading	War Diary of 60th Divisional Sanitary Section From 1st August 1916 To 31st August 1916 (Sheets 1 To 10)		
War Diary	60th Divl. Area	01/08/1916	01/08/1916
War Diary	Hermaville	01/08/1916	01/08/1916
War Diary	Hautes Avesnes	01/08/1916	01/08/1916
War Diary	60th Divl. Area	02/08/1916	02/08/1916
War Diary	Hermaville	02/08/1916	02/08/1916
War Diary	Frevin Capelle	02/08/1916	02/08/1916
War Diary	Etrun	02/08/1916	02/08/1916
War Diary	60th Divl. Area	03/08/1916	03/08/1916
War Diary	Bray Ecoivres	03/08/1916	03/08/1916
War Diary	Frevin Capelle	03/08/1916	03/08/1916
War Diary	Hermaville	03/08/1916	03/08/1916
War Diary	60th Divl. Area	04/08/1916	04/08/1916
War Diary	Hermaville	04/08/1916	04/08/1916
War Diary	Acq Laresset	05/08/1916	05/08/1916
War Diary	Hermaville	05/08/1916	05/08/1916
War Diary	Frevin Capelle	05/08/1916	05/08/1916
War Diary	Hermaville	06/08/1916	07/08/1916
War Diary	Etrun	07/08/1916	07/08/1916
War Diary	60th Divl. Area	08/08/1916	08/08/1916
War Diary	Hermaville	08/08/1916	08/08/1916
War Diary	Mt St Eloy	08/08/1916	08/08/1916
War Diary	Etrun	09/08/1916	09/08/1916
War Diary	Divl. Area	09/08/1916	09/08/1916
War Diary	Hautes Avesnes	09/08/1916	09/08/1916
War Diary	Mont St. Eloy	09/08/1916	09/08/1916
War Diary	Frevin Capelle	09/08/1916	09/08/1916

War Diary	Hermaville		09/08/1916	09/08/1916
War Diary	60th Divl. Area		10/08/1916	10/08/1916
War Diary	Hautes Avesnes		10/08/1916	10/08/1916
War Diary	Hermaville		10/08/1916	10/08/1916
War Diary	60th Divl. Area		11/08/1916	11/08/1916
War Diary	Hermaville		11/08/1916	11/08/1916
War Diary	Ecoivres		11/08/1916	11/08/1916
War Diary	Haute-Avesnes Frevin-Capelle Ecoivres		11/08/1916	11/08/1916
War Diary	Frevin Capelle		12/08/1916	12/08/1916
War Diary	Hermaville		12/08/1916	13/08/1916
War Diary	60th Divl. Area		14/08/1916	14/08/1916
War Diary	Ecoivres		14/08/1916	14/08/1916
War Diary	Frevin Capelle		14/08/1916	14/08/1916
War Diary	Hermaville		14/08/1916	14/08/1916
War Diary	Etrun		14/08/1916	14/08/1916
War Diary	60th Divl. Area		15/08/1916	15/08/1916
War Diary	Ecoivres		15/08/1916	15/08/1916
War Diary	Hermaville		15/08/1916	15/08/1916
War Diary	60th Divl. Area		16/08/1916	16/08/1916
War Diary	Maroeuil		16/08/1916	16/08/1916
War Diary	Etrun		16/08/1916	16/08/1916
War Diary	60th Div. Area		17/08/1916	17/08/1916
War Diary	Frevin Capelle		17/08/1916	17/08/1916
War Diary	Ecoivres		17/08/1916	17/08/1916
War Diary	Hermaville		17/08/1916	17/08/1916
War Diary	Bray Ecoivres		17/08/1916	17/08/1916
War Diary	60 Divl Area		18/08/1916	18/08/1916
War Diary	Maroeuil		18/08/1916	18/08/1916
War Diary	Ecoivres		18/08/1916	18/08/1916
War Diary	Laresset		18/08/1916	18/08/1916
War Diary	Hermaville		18/08/1916	18/08/1916
War Diary	Haute-Avesnes		18/08/1916	18/08/1916
War Diary	Hermaville		19/08/1916	20/08/1916
War Diary	60th Div. Area		21/08/1916	21/08/1916
War Diary	Hermaville		21/08/1916	21/08/1916
War Diary	Acq		21/08/1916	21/08/1916
War Diary	60th Divl. Area		22/08/1916	22/08/1916
War Diary	Etrun		22/08/1916	22/08/1916
War Diary	Hermaville		22/08/1916	22/08/1916
War Diary	60th Divl. Area		23/08/1916	23/08/1916
War Diary	Sur St Michel		23/08/1916	23/08/1916
War Diary	Hermaville		23/08/1916	23/08/1916
War Diary	60th Divl. Area		24/08/1916	24/08/1916
War Diary	St. Michel		24/08/1916	24/08/1916
War Diary	Laresset		24/08/1916	24/08/1916
War Diary	Hermaville		24/08/1916	24/08/1916
War Diary	60th Divl. Area		25/08/1916	25/08/1916
War Diary	Frevin Capelle		25/08/1916	25/08/1916
War Diary	Hermaville		25/08/1916	25/08/1916
War Diary	Ecoivres Frevin Capelle		25/08/1916	25/08/1916
War Diary	Hermaville		26/08/1916	27/08/1916
War Diary	60th Divl Area		28/08/1916	28/08/1916
War Diary	Mont St Eloy		28/08/1916	28/08/1916
War Diary	Laresset		28/08/1916	28/08/1916
War Diary	Maroeuil		28/08/1916	28/08/1916
War Diary	Hermaville		28/08/1916	28/08/1916

War Diary	60th Divl Area	29/08/1916	29/08/1916
War Diary	Etrun	29/08/1916	29/08/1916
War Diary	St. Michel	29/08/1916	29/08/1916
War Diary	Hermaville	30/08/1916	30/08/1916
War Diary	Divl. Area	30/08/1916	30/08/1916
War Diary	Tilloy	31/08/1916	31/08/1916
War Diary	Ecoivres	31/08/1916	31/08/1916
War Diary	Hermaville	31/08/1916	31/08/1916
Heading	War Diary of Sanitary Section 60th (London) Division From 1st September 1916 To 30th September 1916 Volume X		
War Diary	60th Divl. Area	01/09/1916	01/09/1916
War Diary	Maroeuil	01/09/1916	01/09/1916
War Diary	Hermaville	01/09/1916	01/09/1916
War Diary	Etrun	02/09/1916	02/09/1916
War Diary	Hermaville	02/09/1916	03/09/1916
War Diary	Divl. Area	04/09/1916	04/09/1916
War Diary	Hermaville	04/09/1916	04/09/1916
War Diary	Bray	04/09/1916	04/09/1916
War Diary	Larasset	04/09/1916	04/09/1916
War Diary	Ecoivres	04/09/1916	04/09/1916
War Diary	Mt. St. Eloy	04/09/1916	04/09/1916
War Diary	Frevin Capelle	04/09/1916	04/09/1916
War Diary	Divl. Area	05/09/1916	05/09/1916
War Diary	Hermaville	05/09/1916	05/09/1916
War Diary	Etrun	05/09/1916	05/09/1916
War Diary	Divl Area	06/09/1916	06/09/1916
War Diary	Bray	06/09/1916	06/09/1916
War Diary	Hermaville	06/09/1916	06/09/1916
War Diary	Ecoivres	06/09/1916	06/09/1916
War Diary	Etrun	06/09/1916	06/09/1916
War Diary	Divl. Area	07/09/1916	07/09/1916
War Diary	Larasset	07/09/1916	07/09/1916
War Diary	Hermaville	07/09/1916	07/09/1916
War Diary	Haute Avesnes	07/09/1916	07/09/1916
War Diary	Ecoivres	07/09/1916	07/09/1916
War Diary	Bray	07/09/1916	07/09/1916
War Diary	Etrun	07/09/1916	07/09/1916
War Diary	Divl. Area	08/09/1916	08/09/1916
War Diary	Maroeuil	08/09/1916	08/09/1916
War Diary	Frevin Capelle	08/09/1916	08/09/1916
War Diary	Hermaville	08/09/1916	08/09/1916
War Diary	Ecoivres	08/09/1916	08/09/1916
War Diary	Larasset	08/09/1916	08/09/1916
War Diary	Hermaville	09/09/1916	10/09/1916
War Diary	Frevin Cappelle	11/09/1916	11/09/1916
War Diary	Ecoivres	11/09/1916	11/09/1916
War Diary	Hermaville	11/09/1916	11/09/1916
War Diary	Divl. Area	12/09/1916	12/09/1916
War Diary	Frevin Cappelle	12/09/1916	12/09/1916
War Diary	Ecoivres	12/09/1916	12/09/1916
War Diary	Hermaville	12/09/1916	12/09/1916
War Diary	Bray	12/09/1916	12/09/1916
War Diary	Divl. Area	13/09/1916	13/09/1916
War Diary	Larasset	13/09/1916	13/09/1916
War Diary	Ecoivres	13/09/1916	13/09/1916

War Diary	Maroeuil	13/09/1916	13/09/1916
War Diary	Hermaville	13/09/1916	13/09/1916
War Diary	Divl. Area	14/09/1916	14/09/1916
War Diary	Bray	14/09/1916	14/09/1916
War Diary	Mt St Eloy	14/09/1916	14/09/1916
War Diary	Larasset	14/09/1916	14/09/1916
War Diary	Divl. Area	15/09/1916	15/09/1916
War Diary	Hautes Avesnes	15/09/1916	15/09/1916
War Diary	Bray	15/09/1916	15/09/1916
War Diary	Hermaville	15/09/1916	15/09/1916
War Diary	Hautes Avesnes	16/09/1916	16/09/1916
War Diary	Hermaville	16/09/1916	17/09/1916
War Diary	Divl. Area	18/09/1916	18/09/1916
War Diary	Hermaville	18/09/1916	18/09/1916
War Diary	Divl Area	19/09/1916	19/09/1916
War Diary	Mt St Eloy	19/09/1916	19/09/1916
War Diary	Ecoivres	19/09/1916	19/09/1916
War Diary	Hermaville	19/09/1916	20/09/1916
War Diary	Lillers	20/09/1916	20/09/1916
War Diary	Hermaville	21/09/1916	23/09/1916
War Diary	La Gorgue	23/09/1916	23/09/1916
War Diary	Hermaville	24/09/1916	24/09/1916
War Diary	Divl. Area	25/09/1916	25/09/1916
War Diary	Bray	25/09/1916	25/09/1916
War Diary	Ecoivres	25/09/1916	25/09/1916
War Diary	Hermaville	25/09/1916	25/09/1916
War Diary	Hautes Avesnes	25/09/1916	25/09/1916
War Diary	Ecoivres	25/09/1916	25/09/1916
War Diary	Divl. Area	26/09/1916	26/09/1916
War Diary	Hermaville	26/09/1916	26/09/1916
War Diary	Larasset	26/09/1916	26/09/1916
War Diary	Ecoivres	26/09/1916	26/09/1916
War Diary	Maroeuil	26/09/1916	26/09/1916
War Diary	Divl. Area	27/09/1916	27/09/1916
War Diary	Acq	27/09/1916	27/09/1916
War Diary	Frevin Capelle	27/09/1916	27/09/1916
War Diary	Larasset	27/09/1916	27/09/1916
War Diary	Etrun	27/09/1916	27/09/1916
War Diary	Divl. Area	28/09/1916	28/09/1916
War Diary	Hermaville	28/09/1916	28/09/1916
War Diary	Hautes Avesnes	28/09/1916	28/09/1916
War Diary	Ecoivres	28/09/1916	28/09/1916
War Diary	Divl. Area	29/09/1916	29/09/1916
War Diary	Bray	29/09/1916	29/09/1916
War Diary	Mt St Eloy	29/09/1916	29/09/1916
War Diary	Etrun	29/09/1916	29/09/1916
War Diary	Hermaville	29/09/1916	29/09/1916
War Diary	Ecoivres	29/09/1916	29/09/1916
War Diary	Maroeuil	29/09/1916	29/09/1916
War Diary	Hermaville	30/09/1916	30/09/1916
Heading	60th Divl. Sany Section Oct 1916		
Heading	War Diary of Sanitary Section 60th (London) Division From 1st October 1916 To 31st October 1916		
War Diary	Hermaville	01/10/1916	02/10/1916
War Diary	Frevin Capelle	02/10/1916	02/10/1916
War Diary	Bray	02/10/1916	02/10/1916

War Diary	Ecoivres	02/10/1916	02/10/1916
War Diary	Hautes Avesnes	02/10/1916	02/10/1916
War Diary	Mt St Eloy	02/10/1916	02/10/1916
War Diary	Hermaville	03/10/1916	03/10/1916
War Diary	Mt St Eloy	03/10/1916	03/10/1916
War Diary	Frevin Capelle	03/10/1916	03/10/1916
War Diary	Hautes Avesnes	03/10/1916	03/10/1916
War Diary	Etrun Hermaville	03/10/1916	04/10/1916
War Diary	Aubigny Etrun Hermaville	04/10/1916	05/10/1916
War Diary	Maroeuil Etrun Ecoivres	05/10/1916	05/10/1916
War Diary	Hermaville	06/10/1916	06/10/1916
War Diary	Mt St Eloy	06/10/1916	06/10/1916
War Diary	Etrun	06/10/1916	06/10/1916
War Diary	Bray	06/10/1916	06/10/1916
War Diary	Maroeuil	06/10/1916	06/10/1916
War Diary	Acq Capelle Fermont Hermaville	06/10/1916	06/10/1916
War Diary	Aubigny	07/10/1916	07/10/1916
War Diary	Hautes Avesnes	07/10/1916	07/10/1916
War Diary	Maroeuil Etrun	07/10/1916	07/10/1916
War Diary	Hermaville	08/10/1916	08/10/1916
War Diary	Aubigny	08/10/1916	08/10/1916
War Diary	Hermaville	09/10/1916	09/10/1916
War Diary	Ecoivres	09/10/1916	09/10/1916
War Diary	Mt St Eloy	09/10/1916	09/10/1916
War Diary	Frevin Cappelle	09/10/1916	09/10/1916
War Diary	Cappelle Fermont	09/10/1916	09/10/1916
War Diary	Bray	09/10/1916	09/10/1916
War Diary	Acq	09/10/1916	09/10/1916
War Diary	Ecoivres Haute Avesnes	09/10/1916	09/10/1916
War Diary	Laresset	09/10/1916	09/10/1916
War Diary	Hautes Avesnes	09/10/1916	09/10/1916
War Diary	Hermaville	10/10/1916	10/10/1916
War Diary	Hautes Avesnes	10/10/1916	10/10/1916
War Diary	Ecoivres Maroeuil Haute Avesnes	10/10/1916	10/10/1916
War Diary	Hermaville	11/10/1916	12/10/1916
War Diary	Etrun	12/10/1916	12/10/1916
War Diary	Aubigny	12/10/1916	12/10/1916
War Diary	Hautes Avesnes	12/10/1916	12/10/1916
War Diary	Maroeuil Etrun	12/10/1916	12/10/1916
War Diary	Hermaville	13/10/1916	13/10/1916
War Diary	Acq	13/10/1916	13/10/1916
War Diary	Hermaville	13/10/1916	13/10/1916
War Diary	Mt St. Eloi Ecoivres	13/10/1916	13/10/1916
War Diary	Hermaville	14/10/1916	14/10/1916
War Diary	Hautes Avesnes	14/10/1916	14/10/1916
War Diary	Aubigny Fermont Capelle	14/10/1916	14/10/1916
War Diary	Hermaville	15/10/1916	16/10/1916
War Diary	Ecoivres	16/10/1916	16/10/1916
War Diary	Frevin Cappelle	16/10/1916	16/10/1916
War Diary	Hautes Avesnes	16/10/1916	16/10/1916
War Diary	Etrun Maroeuil	16/10/1916	16/10/1916
War Diary	Hermaville	17/10/1916	17/10/1916
War Diary	Bray	17/10/1916	17/10/1916
War Diary	Aubigny	17/10/1916	17/10/1916
War Diary	Ecoivres	17/10/1916	17/10/1916
War Diary	Hermaville	18/10/1916	18/10/1916

War Diary	Ecoivres Mt St Eloy ACQ Bray Frevent	18/10/1916	18/10/1916
War Diary	Hermaville	19/10/1916	19/10/1916
War Diary	La Couroy	19/10/1916	19/10/1916
War Diary	Hermaville	20/10/1916	20/10/1916
War Diary	Lillers	20/10/1916	20/10/1916
War Diary	Hermaville	21/10/1916	21/10/1916
War Diary	Ecoivres Maroeuil	21/10/1916	21/10/1916
War Diary	Hermaville	22/10/1916	23/10/1916
War Diary	Le Couruy	23/10/1916	23/10/1916
War Diary	St. Pol	23/10/1916	23/10/1916
War Diary	Hermaville	24/10/1916	24/10/1916
War Diary	Le Couray	24/10/1916	24/10/1916
War Diary	Hermaville	24/10/1916	25/10/1916
War Diary	Houvin Houvigneul	25/10/1916	25/10/1916
War Diary	Hermaville	26/10/1916	26/10/1916
War Diary	Houvin-Houvigneul	26/10/1916	28/10/1916
War Diary	Frohen-Le-Grande	28/10/1916	29/10/1916
War Diary	Bernaville	29/10/1916	31/10/1916
Heading	War Diary of 60th Divisional Sanitary Section From 1st November 1916 To 30th November 1916		
War Diary	Bernaville	01/11/1916	03/11/1916
War Diary	Ailly-Le-Haute Clocher	03/11/1916	05/11/1916
War Diary	Divl. Area	05/11/1916	05/11/1916
War Diary	Ailly-Le-H-C Bussus	05/11/1916	08/11/1916
War Diary	Ailly-L-H-C Bussus	08/11/1916	08/11/1916
War Diary	Ailly-Le-Haute Clocher	09/11/1916	09/11/1916
War Diary	Bellancourt	09/11/1916	09/11/1916
War Diary	Ailly-L-H-C	10/11/1916	10/11/1916
War Diary	Vauchelles-Les-Quesnoy	10/11/1916	10/11/1916
War Diary	Ailly-L-H-C	11/11/1916	11/11/1916
War Diary	Buigny L'Abbe	11/11/1916	11/11/1916
War Diary	Ailly-L-H-C	12/11/1916	12/11/1916
War Diary	Buigny L'Abbe	12/11/1916	12/11/1916
War Diary	Ailly-L-H-C	13/11/1916	13/11/1916
War Diary	Eaucourt	13/11/1916	13/11/1916
War Diary	Ailly-L-H-C	14/11/1916	14/11/1916
War Diary	Eaucourt	14/11/1916	14/11/1916
War Diary	Ailly-Le-Haute-Clocher	15/11/1916	15/11/1916
War Diary	Brucamps	15/11/1916	15/11/1916
War Diary	Ailly-L-H-C	15/11/1916	16/11/1916
War Diary	Brucamps	16/11/1916	16/11/1916
War Diary	Ergnies	16/11/1916	16/11/1916
War Diary	Gorenflos	16/11/1916	16/11/1916
War Diary	Ailly-Le-Haute-Clocher	17/11/1916	17/11/1916
War Diary	Bussus Ergnies	17/11/1916	17/11/1916
War Diary	Ailly-Le-Haute-Clocher	18/11/1916	18/11/1916
War Diary	Yaucourt	18/11/1916	18/11/1916
War Diary	Gorenflos	18/11/1916	18/11/1916
War Diary	Villers-Sous-Ailly	18/11/1916	19/11/1916
War Diary	Moufflers	19/11/1916	19/11/1916
War Diary	Gorenflos	19/11/1916	19/11/1916
War Diary	Divl. Area	20/11/1916	20/11/1916
War Diary	Vauchelles-Les-Domarts	20/11/1916	20/11/1916
War Diary	Divl Area	21/11/1916	21/11/1916
War Diary	Vauchelles-Les-Domart	21/11/1916	21/11/1916
War Diary	Ailly-Le-Haute-Clocher	22/11/1916	24/11/1916

War Diary	Longpre	24/11/1916	24/11/1916
War Diary	Montereau	25/11/1916	25/11/1916
War Diary	Macon	26/11/1916	26/11/1916
War Diary	Pierrelatte	26/11/1916	26/11/1916
War Diary	Marseilles	27/11/1916	30/11/1916

WO 95/30209

60TH DIVISION

SANITARY SECTION

~~JUN - NOV 1916~~

1916 FEB - 1916 NOV

Confidential.

War Diary

of

Sanitary Section 60th (London) Div'n.

from 29th Feb'ry 1916. to

(Volume 1.)

3 Appendices
"A", "B" & "C".

5 Sheets.

4 Sheets

Army Form C. 2118

WAR DIARY
~~INTELLIGENCE SUMMARY~~
(Erase heading not required.)

SANITARY SECTION
60th (LONDON) DIVISION

(1)

Instructions regarding War Diaries and Intelligence Summaries are contained in F.S. Regs., Part II. and the Staff Manual respectively. Title Pages will be prepared in manuscript.

Place	Date 1916	Hour	Summary of Events and Information	Remarks and references to Appendices
SUTTON VENY	Feb. 29	3-20 pm	Arrived at Warminster:— Lieut. H.S. Tebbutt. O.C. 27 Other Ranks. 3 ton Daimler Lorry (5474) "Y" type and Equipment. 1 Horse. Reported to D.A.D.M.S. 60th (London) Division for duty as Divisional Sanitary Section. Quartered:— O.C. at Divisional Headquarters. Daimler Motor Lorry do do Horse do do N.C.O.s and men at Hut 30. Camp 6.	See A (1 sheet)
do	do 2		Drew Hut furniture & stores from O/i/c. Barracks. Fitted up Orderly Room in Hut 30. Camp 6.	
do	do 3	10 a.m.	No. 2978. Pte. H. Horn admitted to SUTTON VENY Military Hospital (Scabies)	
do	March 4th to 10th		Detailed 20. N.C.O.s and men to make Daily Inspections of Divisional Camps — dividing the area dealt with into Seven Districts for this purpose. Made a return of Divisional Incinerators and their condition.	See B (3 sheets)
do	March 11th	2 pm	Continued Daily District Inspections. No. 2976. Pte. R. Horn discharged from SUTTON VENY M. Hospital to duty.	H.S.T.

1875 Wt. W593/826 1,000,000 4/15 J.B.C. & A. A.D.S.S./Forms/C. 2118.

Army Form C. 2118

(2)

WAR DIARY
~~INTELLIGENCE SUMMARY~~
SANITARY SECTION
60th (LONDON) DIVISION
(Erase heading not required.)

Instructions regarding War Diaries and Intelligence Summaries are contained in F.S. Regs., Part II and the Staff Manual respectively. Title Pages will be prepared in manuscript.

Place	Date 1916.	Hour	Summary of Events and Information	Remarks and references to Appendices
SUTTON VENY.	March 13th to March 31st		Continued Daily District Inspections.	
	April 1 to April 5		Continued Daily District Inspections.	
	April 6th to April 12th		Made approach road to Divisional Manure tip in Heytesbury Rd.	
	April 13th to 17th		Continued Daily District Inspections.	
	April 18th 9-30 AM		No 2978 Pte R Hern admitted to SUTTON VENY Military Hospital (Disease No 736.)	
	April 18th to 29th		Continued Daily District Inspections.	
	April 29th		Moved from Hut 30. Camp. 6. to Hut 30 + 38. Camp 9. SUTTON VENY.	
	May 2nd		Revised District Sanitary Inspection areas owing to Moves of Divisional Units.	See "C" (1 sheet) H-S.T.
	May 3rd		Continued Daily District Inspections.	

1875 Wt. W593/325 1,000,000 4/15 J.B.C. & A. A.D.S.S./Forms/C. 2118. —

Army Form C. 2118

WAR DIARY
or
INTELLIGENCE SUMMARY
(Erase heading not required.)

SANITARY SECTION
60th (LONDON) DIVISION

(3)

Place	Date 1916	Hour	Summary of Events and Information	Remarks and references to Appendices
SUTTON VENY.	May 1st to May 22nd		Continued Daily District Inspections.	
	May 23rd		Divisional Route March and Inspection by I.G.C.	
	May 24th			
	May 25th & 26th		Continued Daily District Inspections.	
	May 27th		Received from A.S.C. M.T. Depot One 3.cwt. Rifle for transport Lorry.	
	May 27th		Continued Daily District Inspections.	
	May 30th		Reviewed by H.M. King George V.	
	May 31st		Continued Daily District Inspections.	
	June 1st		3064 Sept Retro, W.H.S. transferred to 2/2nd London Sanitary Coy (at Richmond)	
	June 2nd		Continued Daily District Inspections.	
	June 3rd		3190 Pte Scarfe, H reported for duty from 1/2nd Ln. Sanitary Coy in place of 2978/26 Wm Cottill in Bulford Hospital	
	June 4th to June 7th		Continued Daily District Inspections.	
	June 8th to June 13th		do do do	
	June 14th		2978 Pte Herne, H. discharged from Bulford Hospital	

Army Form C. 2118

WAR DIARY
or
INTELLIGENCE SUMMARY
(Erase heading not required.)

SANITARY SECTION
60th (LONDON) DIVISION

Instructions regarding War Diaries and Intelligence Summaries are contained in F.S. Regs., Part II. and the Staff Manual respectively. Title Pages will be prepared in manuscript.

Place	Date 1916	Hour	Summary of Events and Information	Remarks and references to Appendices
SUTTON VENY	June 15th to June 17th		Continued Daily District Inspections.	
	June 18th		No. 2978. Pte. Henn, R. classified DIII by Standing Medical Board. Latter placed under orders for Overseas — B.E.F.	
	June 19th		Continued Daily District Inspections.	
	June 20th		Inspected Kit, Equipment, Clothing and Stores preparatory to proceeding Overseas.	
	June 21st		Closed Books & Ledgers & forwarded documents as per para. 189. Mob. No. 2978. Pte. Henn, R. transferred to O.C. Details, Medical Units Regt. at No. 9 Camp, Sutton Veny.	

H.S. Tebbutt Lieut.
O.C. SANITARY SECTION
60th (LONDON) DIVISION

29/2/16.

Appendix A.
War Diary. 60th Division

Nominal Roll of Sanitary Section No. 32

Officer in command, Lieut. H.S. Tebbitt.

Reg. No.	Rank.	Name.	Date of Attestation.	Age on Attestation.
2790	S/Sgt.	Neil, D.M.	4. 8.15.	31.6.
3034	Sgt.	Merck, T.H.	29.10.15.	33
2927	Cpl.	Thomas, E.M.	5. 7.15.	32.9.
2735	"	Grinsted, H.A.	14. 7.15.	32.6.
2976	L/Cpl.	Carment, J.M.	18.10.15.	35
3116	Pte.	Abelson, I.	8.11.15.	29.3.
3039	"	Blackaby, S.H.	29.10.15.	28.3.
2784	"	Chinnery, F.T.	3. 8.15.	27.6.
3058	"	Earl, A.B.H.	1.11.15.	28
3061	"	Franklin, H.J.	1.11.15.	37.6.
3008	"	Green, E.J.	25.10.15.	32.6.
3049	"	Hensby, G.H.T.	1.11.15.	34.1.
2931	"	Hargreaves, F.R.	5. 8.15.	26
2978	"	Hern, R.	20.10.15.	32
3007	"	Kelley, A.E.	25.10.15.	19.4.
2975	"	Lovesey, L.	18.10.15.	22.3.
2995	"	Mason, W.N.	25.10.15.	26.8.
2961	"	Morrissey, C.S.	15.10.15.	23
2972	"	Morton, J.H.	18.10.15.	22.5.
3022	"	Mangold, C.F.W.	26.10.15.	25.8.
3020	"	Matthews, W.H.E.	26.10.15.	34
3064	"	Peters, W.F.D.	1.11.15.	35.6.
3063	"	Sillitoe, F.H.C.	1.11.15.	39.
3048	"	Samuel, P.	1.11.15.	26
3028	"	Walls, H.W.	28.10.15.	23.4.
A.S.C. D.M./2/ 138000	Dvr.	Jarritt, W.	26.11.15.	30.3.
D.M./2/ 137864	"	Huggett, H.G.	15.11.15.	23

SANITARY SECTION
60th (LONDON) DIVISION

SANITARY SECTION
60th (LONDON) DIVISION

Appendisc B. (3 sheets.)

3/3/16.

War Diary.

(I.) Sanitary Section — 60th London Division

Allotment of H.Q. and Units for Sanitary Inspection.

Unit.	Address.	N.C.O. and men detailed.
DISTRICT I.		
Divisional Headquarters		Cpl. Merck
G.S.O.(1) G.S.O.(2) G.S.O.(3)		Pte. Hensby.
A.A+Q.M.G. D.A.A+Q.M.G.	Greenhill	
D.A.Q.M.G. A.P.M.	Sutton Veny.	
A.D.V.S. D.A.D.O.S.		
Divisional Manure Dump.		
DISTRICT II.		
H.Q. 179th Infantry Brigade	Longbridge Deverill	
2/13th Battn. London Regiment	Sutton Veny Camp No. 8	Cpl. Thomas
2/14th " " "	" " " " 9	Pte. Abelson
2/15th " " "	Longbridge Deverill Camp No 14	- Morrissey
2/16th " " "	" " " " 13	
2/4th London Field Ambulance	" " " " 14	
DISTRICT III.		
H.Q. 180th Infantry Brigade	Sutton Veny	
2/17th Battn. London Regiment	" - Camp No. 5	Cpl. Grinsted
2/18th " " "	" " " 6	Pte. Matthews
2/19th " " "	" " " 7	- Mangold.
2/20th " " "	" " " 10	
2/5th London Field Ambulance	" " " 7	
DISTRICT IV		
H.Q. 181st Infantry Brigade	Sutton Veny.	
2/21st Battn. London Regiment	" - Camp No 1	L/Cpl. Carment
2/22nd " " "	" " " 2	Pte. Lovesey.
2/23rd " " "	" " " 3	
2/24th " " "	" " " 4	
2/6th London Field Ambulance	" " " 2	

Sheet 1.
App. B. War Diary
3/3/16.

Unit.	Address.	N.C.O. and men detailed
DISTRICT V.		
C.R.A.	Elm Lodge, Sutton Veny.	
2/5th London Brigade R.F.A.	Boyton Camp No. 3	
2/12th County of London Battery	" " " 3	
2/13th " " " "	" " " 3	
2/14th " " " "	" " " 3	Pte Franklin
Ammunition Column.	" " " 3	" Morton
2/6th London Brigade R.F.A.	" " " 1	" Sillitoe
2/15th County of London Battery	" " " 1	" Walls
2/16th " " " "	" " " 1	
2/17th " " " "	" " " 1	
Ammunition Column.	" " " 1	
2/7th London Brigade R.F.A.	" " " 4	
2/18th County of London Battery	" " " 4	
2/19th " " " "	" " " 4	
2/20th " " " "	" " " 4	
Ammunition Column	" " " 4	
2/8th London (How.) Brigade R.F.A.	" " " 2	
2/21st County of London Battery	" " " 2	
2/22nd " " " "	" " " 2	
Ammunition Column	" " " 2	
60th Mobile Veterinary Section	" " " 2	
H.Q. Coy. Divisional Train A.S.C.	Corton	
DISTRICT VI		
C.R.E.	Sutton Veny Camp No. 6	Pte Peters
2/3rd London Field Company	" " " 6	" Earl
2/4th " " "	" " " 6	" Hern
1/6th " " "	" " " 6	
60th (London) Signal Company	" " " 7	
60th (London) Cyclists Company	" " " 7	
A.D.M.S.	" " " 6	
60th London Casualty Clearing Station	" " " 5	
DISTRICT VII		
H.Q. 60th (London) Divisional Train	Warminster North Camp	
179th Bde.	" "	Pte Hargreaves
180th "	" "	" Golew
181st "	" "	" Blacksby
Senior Supply Officer	South Camp	
58th Field Butchery	" "	
67th Field Bakery	" "	
294-298 Depot. Units of Supply.	" "	

Sheet 2.
App. B. War Diary
3/3/16

SANITARY SECTION
60th (LONDON) DIVISION

Instructions for Sanitary Inspection.

(II.)

The duties of a Section-man in charge of a Unit will be as follows:—

(a) To make a daily inspection of all Cookhouses, Washhouses, Latrines, Urinals, Incinerators, and Horse Lines in the area occupied by his Unit.

(b) To keep a Diary of visits and inspections made.

(c) To make a report to the Orderly Room of any matters calling for immediate attention.

(d) To hand in to the Orderly Room every Friday evening a report of the work carried out during the week.

(III.)

The following are the chief points to be observed in making an inspection, and to be used as headings when a report is to be made:—

Cookhouses. — Disposal of waste matter — Grease traps — General cleanliness of interior and of surroundings.

Wash Houses — Description — Disposal of waste water — General sanitary condition.

Latrines and Urinals. — Number and description — Disposal of excreta and urine. — General sanitary condition.

Incinerator — Type and description. — Working condition — Storage of unburnt refuse — Disposal of burnt refuse — Condition of surroundings.

Horse Lines. — Description — Storage and disposal of manure — General sanitary condition.

Sheet 3.
App. B. War Diary
3/3/16
O.C. H J Tebbutt. Lieut
SANITARY SECTION
60th (LONDON) DIVISION

(1 Sheet)

Appendix "C" of 1st May 1916.

War Diary

60th (London) Divisional Sanitary Section

Revision of Allotment of H.Q. and Units of 60th Division for Sanitary Inspection.

District No 1.   Sgt J. H. Merck
    Additions   Rifle Ranges A.B.C & D Longbridge Deverill Road
                  Camp No 9 All 60th Divisional Medical Units
    Reduction   Divisional Manure Dump Heytesbury Road

District No 2.
    Reduction. Camp 14. 2/4th London Field Amb̄   Cpl. E. M. Thomas + 1 Other

District No 3.   Cpl H. A. Grinsted + 1 Other
    Reduction. Camp 7. 2/5th London Field Amb̄

District No 4.   L/Cpl. Garment + 1 Other
    Reduction. Camp 2. 2/6th London Field Amb̄

District No 5.   L/Cpl Franklin + 3 Others
    Addition. Divisional Manure Dump. Corton Road

District No 6.   L/Cpl. Peters + 2 Others
    Reduction. Camp 5. 60th London Divl Cas. Clearing Stn

District No 7   Pte Green + 1 other
    Unchanged

District No 8
    (New District)   L/Cpl Hargreaves + 2 others
       Divisional Manure Dump Heytesbury Road
       No 3 Camp 1/1st Hampshire Yeomanry   H.S.T
        Heytesbury

Original.

Confidential.

War Diary of
Sanitary Section
60th Division B.E.F.

from:- 27th June 1916. to 31st July 1916.

(8 Sheets.)

MEDICAL.

SANITARY SECTION
60th (LONDON) DIVISION

Army Form C. 2118

WAR DIARY
or
INTELLIGENCE SUMMARY
(Erase heading not required.)

No. 1

Instructions regarding War Diaries and Intelligence Summaries are contained in F.S. Regs., Part II. and the Staff Manual respectively. Title Pages will be prepared in manuscript.

Place	Date	Hour	Summary of Events and Information	Remarks and references to Appendices
SUTTON VENY	27/6/16	4-30 a.m.	Paraded all ranks (600/pl Transport which had previously left) Marched to WARMINSTER	A.S.T
		6-20	Entrained	
SOUTHAMPTON	do	9-0	Detrained at SOUTHAMPTON	A.S.T
		4-30 p.m.	Embarked on "S.S HUNSLET" with Transport & Stores.	
		6-0 p.m.	Sailed.	
LE HAVRE	25/6/16	7-0 a.m.	Disembarked, & unloaded Transport & Stores.	A.S.T
do	do	2-0 p.m.	Marched to SANVIC Rest Camp No. 2	
	26/6/16	5-0 a.m.	to Station, despatched Transport by Road and Entrained leaving at 9-30 a.m.	A.S.T
ABBEVILLE	do	8-30 p.m.	½ hour halt on Rail journey	
PETIT HOUVIN	27/6/16	2-0 a.m.	Detrained and marched to Billet at FLERS	A.S.T
LE FLERS	28/6/16	12-30 midday	By Lorry to VILLERS CHATEL & quartered at Billet No. 25.	A.S.T
VILLERS CHATTEL	29/6/16		VILLERS CHATEL divided into 4 Sanitary Districts including H.Q. Divn. & commenced General Sanitary Inspections supervision & construction of Sanitary necessaries	A.S.T A.S.T
do	30/6/16		Daily District Inspections continued. Inspected Baths at TINQUES & SAVY	A.S.T A.S.T
do	1/7/16 to 5/7/16		Daily District Inspections	A.S.T
do	5/7/16		Carted soiled clothes from TINQUES BATHS to CORPS laundry at ST POL & redelivered clean clothing & Baths	A.S.T
do	6/7/16		Daily District Inspection also detailed to BETHONSART & BETHINCOURT. Inspected Baths at MAROEVIL, ACQ & ECOIVRES	A.S.T
do	7/7/16		Daily District Inspections - Daily Laundry Carting as Periodical Inspection. Lorry taken to A.S.C. M.T. Depot for Lorry Carting on 5th returnt	A.S.T

151

WAR DIARY
or
INTELLIGENCE SUMMARY

(Erase heading not required.)

SANITARY SECTION
60th (LONDON) DIVISION Army Form C. 2118

No. 2

Place	Date	Hour	Summary of Events and Information	Remarks and references to Appendices
VILLERS CHATEL	8/7/16 to 13/7/16		Daily District Inspections. CAMBLIGNEUL added. " Laundry Centry " do do	MST MST MST MST MST
do	14/7/16	6-30pm	Advance party with Transport & Part of Stores proceeded to Headquarters at HERMAVILLE and took over Billets & Stores & offices from Scottish General Sanitary Section – Nos 71, 5th	MST
		12-noon	84, 92 & 95. RIEDIGER.	
		2 pm	Remainder of Personnel & Stores removed to HERMAVILLE & took over Second.	
HERMAVILLE	15/7/16		Divided HERMAVILLE into Sanitary Districts & proceeded with provision of necessities	MST
do	16/7/16 to 19/7/16		Daily District Inspections and work	MST MST MST MST
do	20/7/16 to 28/7/16		do do do	MST MST MST MST
do	29/7/16 to 31/7/16		Daily District Inspections of HERMAVILLE (with fatigue party averaging 15 men) and HAUTES AVESNES – FREVIN CAPPELLE – ACQ – ECOIVRES – MAROEUIL MONT ST ELOY – BRAY – LARESSET & TILLOY LES HERMAVILLE.	MST MST

H.S. Tebbutt. Capt.
O.C.
SANITARY SECTION
60th (LONDON) DIVISION

Confidential

Medical

August 1916

Vol 3

War Diary

of

60th Divisional Sanitary Section

from 1st August 1916. to 31st August 1916.

(Sheets 1 to 10.)

COMMITTEE FOR THE
MEDICAL HISTORY OF THE WAR
Date -5 OCT. 1916

Medical

Army Form C. 2118

SANITARY SECTION
60th (LONDON) DIVISION

WAR DIARY
or
INTELLIGENCE SUMMARY
(Erase heading not required.)

Instructions regarding War Diaries and Intelligence Summaries are contained in F.S. Regs., Part II. and the Staff Manual respectively. Title Pages will be prepared in manuscript.

Place	Date	Hour	Summary of Events and Information	Remarks and references to Appendices
60th Divl. AREA.	1/8/16		District Inspections of Divisional Units Camps and Billeting Areas.	
HERMAVILLE			Inspected 5 Billets in Rue d'Izel and recommended Sanitary Works before occupation by Divisional reinforcement Drafts	HST
HAUTES-AVESNES			C.O., 5 N.C.Os & men of Section, and convalescent fatigue party (10 men) scavenging roads & billets.	
60th Divl. AREA	2/8/16		District Sanitary Inspections.	
HERMAVILLE			San. Section Sgt. with O.C. fatigue clearing roads and culverts. Disinfected A.D.M.S. Office and Billet 63. (Reinforcements). A.P.M. to Sanitary Works. Billet 65. Latrines and Ablution Bench & Pit. to 63. Latrines. Scavenged Billet 69. Well water at D.A.C. Billet Horrock's Lodge. 3 Con. Coy. fatigue men scavenging generally. C.O. visited 181st & Brigade M.Os. re erection of permanent sanitary works.	
FREVIN CAPELLE				
ETRUN				HST
60th Divl. AREA	3/8/16		District Sanitary Inspections.	
BRAY ECOIVRES			C.O. visited 179th Brigade Rest Camps.	
FREVIN CAPELLE			Disinfected Huts 1 & 2. D.A.C.	HST

Medical

Army Form C. 2118

SANITARY SECTION
60th (LONDON) DIVISION

WAR DIARY
or
INTELLIGENCE SUMMARY
(Erase heading not required.)

Instructions regarding War Diaries and Intelligence Summaries are contained in F.S. Regs., Part II. and the Staff Manual respectively. Title Pages will be prepared in manuscript.

Place	Date	Hour	Summary of Events and Information	Remarks and references to Appendices
HERMAVILLE	3/8/16		Disinfections: Billets No. 4. occupied by M.M.P.	
			do 73. do Bombing School.	
			do 94. for Reinforcement Drafts.	
			do 108. do	
			Barn at do 98. do	
			Road Cleaning: San. Sec. N.C.O. and 10 Con. Coy. fatigue men.	
60th DIV⁴ AREA	4/8/16		District Sanitary Inspections.	A.D.T
HERMAVILLE			Made and fixed 2-breseat latrine with trough urinal at Billet 108.	
			do Ablution bench, grease traps & wood covered leakage pit at 108.	
			Road Cleaning: S. Sec. N.C.O. + Con Coy fatigue party of 6 men.	A.S.I.
A.C.G.	5/8/16		C.O. Visited Town Major re general sanitation. also inspected	
LARESSET			Disinfections:- Billet No. 5. occupied by B300. R.F.A. occupied by 303/B Dup R.F.A.	
HERMAVILLE			Divisional H.Q. 2 Rooms.	
			do Billet No. 5 occupied by B300 R.F.A.	
			Road & Billet yard scavenging throughout Village.	
			Sanitary Works:- Fixed New Latrine complete at yard by H.Q. Farriers Billet No. 49. for French Mission Billet 77 for French Mission Billet 73 Latrine. Made & fixed corrugated iron Incinerator at Billet 73. Bombing School. Repaired: R.E. Signals D.R. Latrine. Billet 73 Latrine. A.D.M.S. Cavalry Latrine.	A.S.I.

Medical

Army Form C. 2118

3

WAR DIARY
or
INTELLIGENCE SUMMARY

SANITARY SECTION LONDON DIVISION

(Erase heading not required.)

Instructions regarding War Diaries and Intelligence Summaries are contained in F.S. Regs., Part II. and the Staff Manual respectively. Title Pages will be prepared in manuscript.

Place	Date	Hour	Summary of Events and Information	Remarks and references to Appendices
FREVIN CAPELLE	5/8/16		San. Sec. N.C.O. & Con. Corp. fatigue party cleaning up D.A.C. Billets. San. Sec. inspects the bricks with C.O. D.A.C.	H.S.T.
HERMAVILLE	6/8/16		General Sanitary Supervision of all H.Q. Billets.	H.S.T.
	7/8/16	6 a.m.	Motor Lorry to A.S.C. Sup. Column M.T. workshops for inspection, returned in evening	
		9 a.m.	Commenced preparation of Sketch Plans of Divisional Sanitary Area for H.Q. XIII Corps Made 2 Ablution Benches for D.A.C. 6 Washing Bowls & delivered to O.C. Corps Corps	
ETRUN		for-noon	10 M.C.O. visits M.O. Battalion — Rest and inspects Billets O.C. visits M.O. of Section and 21 Corps fatigue men arranged all Sheets and Billets. M.O.T.	
60th Div AREA	8/8/16		District Sanitary Inspections Continued Sketch plan of Divisional Sanitary Area.	
HERMAVILLE			Made & fixed new latrine R.A. H.Q. (men) & Lancer	
Mt. ST. ELOI		for-noon	Disinfections: Convalescent Camps Orderly Room & Med. Inspection Room O.C. visits M.O. Batt. in Rest and inspects Camp	A.S.T.
ETRUN	9/8/16	for-noon	C.O. Visited and inspected Sanitary Works	
Div. AREA			District Sanitary Inspections	
HAUTES AVESNES		af-noon	Supervision of Con. Coy. fatigue party clearing up round 2/5th Field Amb. Hospital O.C. was & inspects work in progress	
MONT ST ELOY			Spray of 1 mile of stream with crude oil	
FREVIN CAPELLE			Fixed ablution Benches made for D.A.C. Camp & Repaired Lavatory Bench.	
HERMAVILLE			Continued Sketch plans of Divisional Area.	M.S.T.

1875   Wt. W593/826 1,000,000 4/15 I.B.C. & A.   A.D.S.S./Forms/C. 2118.

Medical

Army Form C. 2118

WAR DIARY
or
INTELLIGENCE SUMMARY
(Erase heading not required.)

SANITARY SECTION
60th (LONDON) DIVISION

Instructions regarding War Diaries and Intelligence Summaries are contained in F.S. Regs., Part II. and the Staff Manual respectively. Title Pages will be prepared in manuscript.

Place	Date	Hour	Summary of Events and Information	Remarks and references to Appendices
60th Divl. AREA	10/8/16		District Sanitary Inspection.	
HAUTES AVESNES			Sanx. Sec., N.C.O. & 3 fatigue near clearing horse lines	
HERMAVILLE			Continued sketch plan of Sanitary Area	H.S.T.
			O.C. insped. all bilts with D.A.D.M.S.	
60th Divl. AREA	11/8/16		District Sanitary Inspection.	
HERMAVILLE			Sanitary Works:- Repaired No.3. H.Q. Mess Officers' Latrine. Made prisoners servants Latrine. Clearing manure heap at No. 63. Billet repapering in Orchard.	
			Disinfections:- A.D.M.S. new office - Billet No. 30. Billet No. 17	
ECOIVRES		all day	1 Sant Sgt + 278 Coy R.E.	H.S.T.
HAUTE-AVESNES FREVIN-CAPELLE ECOIVRES			Inspection of Billets & Camps by D.A.D.M.S. 60th Division and O.C. San Sec.	
FREVIN CAPELLE	12/8/16	a.m. and p.m.	C.O., 7 N.C.O.s, men of duration with fatigue party of 22 men disinfected Billets Nos 2, 3, 5, 8, 9, 10, 12 + 14 for occupation by Entrenching Coy, and One hut for No.3. Section of D.A.C.	
HERMAVILLE			Scavenging with fatigue party:- Roads and Billets	H.S.T.
			Sanitary Works:- Made + fixed new latrine for A.D.M.S at Billet 30. Aluminum Bench for Signals Coy. R.S.	
	13/8/16		General Sanitary Work. Repaired at Billet No. 30. A.D.M.S. Clerk's Latrine.	H.S.T.

Medical

Army Form C. 2118

WAR DIARY
or
INTELLIGENCE SUMMARY
SANITARY SECTION
60th (LONDON) DIVISION

(Erase heading not required.)

Instructions regarding War Diaries and Intelligence Summaries are contained in F.S. Regs., Part II. and the Staff Manual respectively. Title Pages will be prepared in manuscript.

Place	Date	Hour	Summary of Events and Information	Remarks and references to Appendices
60th Div. AREA	14/8/16		District Inspections.	
ECOIVRES		fore-noon	C.O. inspected 2/4th H. Ambce Camp. + interviewed Town Major re sanitation of Billets	
FREVIN CAPELLE			Constructed Latrines for Entrenching Coy.	
			Disinfected Billets 9 + 11 do. do.	
HERMAVILLE			Continued palans of Sanitary Area.	
			Repaired well-cover at Billet No.6.3. & continued cleaning heaps	H.S.T.
ETRUN		after-noon	Made & fixed name-plates for R.E. Dug-out Coy. Billets & obtained permit from Major re sanitation	
			of Civilian M.O. Batt. in Rest + inspected	
60 Kn Div. AREA	15/8/16		District Sanitary Inspections.	
ECOIVRES			C.O. visited Town Major and arranged for fatigue to cleanse Billets.	
HERMAVILLE			Continued revising sanitary area plans.	
			Disinfections: A.D.M.S. Office (2 rooms) & arranged manure in yard.	N.S.T.
			Hut at Grenade School.	
60th Div. AREA	16/8/16		District Sanitary Inspections.	
MAROEUIL			C.O. visited Baths and inspected Foden Lorry Thresh Disinfector placed in charge by A.D.M.S. or nomination of 134th mot. No. 5502. T 5290.	A.S.T.
ETRUN			C.O. inspected 2/2/1st Battn store 2/22 Batt. Kitchens and sanitary work in progress	

Medical

Army Form C. 2118

WAR DIARY or INTELLIGENCE SUMMARY

(Erase heading not required.)

Sanitary Section 60th (London) Division

Instructions regarding War Diaries and Intelligence Summaries are contained in F.S. Regs., Part II. and the Staff Manual respectively. Title Pages will be prepared in manuscript.

Place	Date	Hour	Summary of Events and Information	Remarks and references to Appendices
60th Divl. AREA	17/8/16		District Sanitary Inspections	6
FREVIN CAPELLE			Disinfected:- Billet 13 A. Antrenching Coy.	
			do 49 D.A.C.	
ECOIVRES			Sanitary Works:- Made and fixed Incinerator (Coy) for D.A.C.	
			do do Heavy Artillery	
HERMAVILLE			Disinfection: Postal Clerks Office.	
BRAY ECOIVRES		fore-noon	A.P.M.'s Office.	
			O.C. Trails inspects Camp of Batt. in Rest. — 13th Bn. Transport Lines & 175 Bde Machine Gun Coy.	No 1
60 DIVL. AREA	18/8/16		District Sanitary Inspections	
MARGEVIL			Sprayed with crude oil Midden, Manure heaps and stagnant water at No 13. Argin Rd. - 1, 16 + 26 Avenue Rd. — 25 Ambulance St — 6 Neuville St. 294 Church St. — 7 Bondigue St. — Unnumbered l/w Cemetery Rd & 1/w Cheshire Lane.	
ECOIVRES			Sprayed Midden at Billet 74.	
LARESSET			Disinfected Room at No. 5. — C.O. Trails inspects 301 & 300 F. Bde R.F.A. Lines Billets	
HERMAVILLE		fore-noon	Continued plans of Sanitary Area	
HAUTE. AVESNES			Referred: O.R.A. Officers 60 S.C. Lines about Billets.	No. 1
HERMAVILLE	19/8/16		Continued plans of Sanitary Area	
			Examined Roads & Billets generally	
			O.C. inspects Billets with D.A.D.M.S.	No. 1

Medical

Army Form C. 2118

WAR DIARY
or
INTELLIGENCE SUMMARY
(Erase heading not required.)

SANITARY SECTION
60th (LONDON) DIVISION

Instructions regarding War Diaries and Intelligence Summaries are contained in F.S. Regs., Part II. and the Staff Manual respectively. Title Pages will be prepared in manuscript.

Place	Date	Hour	Summary of Events and Information	Remarks and references to Appendices
HERMAVILLE	19/8/16		Sanitary Works:— Made & fixed N.C.O.s Latrine at R.E. Signals Camp. do. Rough kennel D.A.D.O.S. Store. do. to Billet 65. Reinforcements.	H.O.T.
HERMAVILLE	20/8/16	3 p.m.	Removed Orderly Room from Billet 84 to Billet 73. Sanitary Works:— Made & fixed (From Reservation) at H.Q. Cookhouse by Billet 79. one H.Q. Clerks' Mess do. 116 one D.A.D.O.S. store yard Rue d'Bel one R.E. Signals Camp one Reinforcements Billet No. 65. one	
60th Div. AREA	21/8/16		District Sanitary Inspection.	H.S.
HERMAVILLE			Sanitary Works:— Part rept. to M.O.7. H.Q. Officers' Mess Latrine.	
ACQ.		all day	Completed removal of manure heaps at 63 Billet. Works G. Loose Inspection by O.C.	H.O.T.
60th Div. AREA	22/8/16		C.O. visited M.O. 2/16th Battn. at Bray N Mill Stream. District Sanitary Inspection. C.O. Inspected districts of ETRUN, MAROEUIL & ECOIVRE.	
ETRUN			Repaired 17 Latrine Seats.	
HERMAVILLE			Fatigue party emptying trade and removing detritus.	H.O.T.

1875 Wt. W593/826 1,000,000 4/15 I.B.C. & A. A.D.S.S./Forms/C. 2118.

Medical

Army Form C. 2118

8

WAR DIARY
INTELLIGENCE SUMMARY
(Erase heading not required.)

Instructions regarding War Diaries and Intelligence Summaries are contained in F.S. Regs., Part II. and the Staff Manual respectively. Title Pages will be prepared in manuscript.

Place	Date	Hour	Summary of Events and Information	Remarks and references to Appendices
60th Divl AREA	23/8/16	all day	District Sanitary Inspections.	
SUR ST. MICHEL			C.O. with 2 N.C.O.s & men supervising 3rd Army Re-inforcement Camps Sanitation.	
HERMAVILLE			Continued plans of Sanitary shed. Prepared Models of Sanitary fittings for D.A.D.M.S. Lectures on Sanitation in the Field. Supervised Con. Coy. Fatigue party cleaning RUE d'ARRAS. Made & fixed trough Urinal at No. 63. Billet for Re-inforcements. Sprayed (crude oil) stagnant water at No. 64. A.D.V.S. office. (creso.C) Manure heaps at No. 98.	Ref.
60th Divl AREA	24/8/16	all day	District Sanitary Inspections.	
ST. MICHEL LARESSET HERMAVILLE			C.O. Inspected work at 3rd Army Re-inforcement Camps. Burning Manure heaps for B.300 & 301. Supervising Fatigue parts of Con. Coy. cleaning roads. Emptied Billet No. 3. Preparing Models of Sanitary fittings.	No 6.
60th Divl AREA	25/8/16	all day	District Sanitary Inspections. Burning D.A.C. manure heaps. Making models of Sanitary fittings. Supervising Con. Coy. Fatigue party cleaning roads.	
FREVIN CAPELLE HERMAVILLE				
ECOIVRES FREVIN-CAPELLE			Made & fixed trough Urinal at Grande school. O.E. walls & inspected billets and horse lines	No. 7.

Medical

Army Form C. 2118

WAR DIARY
or
INTELLIGENCE SUMMARY
(Erase heading not required.)

Instructions regarding War Diaries and Intelligence Summaries are contained in F.S. Regs., Part II. and the Staff Manual respectively. Title Pages will be prepared in manuscript.

Place	Date	Hour	Summary of Events and Information	Remarks and references to Appendices
HERMAVILLE	26/8/16		Making Models for D.A.D.M.S. Lecture. M.O.'s fixed new latrine at A.D.M.S. Billet, No.22. Renewed filter at Convalescent Camp Bathhouse. Limewashing cookhouse at 7.S. Billet for Bombing School. Supervised Corps Coy. fatigue party clearing roads & ditches.	Not.
HERMAVILLE	27/8/16		Completed & fixed 8 models for D.A.D.M.S. Lecture.	N.T.
60K.DIV.AREA	28/8/16		C.O. visited 180th Brigade H.Q. re Manure accumulations & infected Batts. in Raoul Camp & billets.	
MONT ST. ELOY			Sprayed (crude oil) Manure heaps 180K. H.Q.	
LARESSET			Made and fixed new latrine for B.301. R.F.A.	
MAROEUIL			Disinfected 14 dugouts in Upper Avenue & Dugouts, Horses & Barns at Bruno Farm.	
HERMAVILLE			Supervised Road cleaning.	N.T.
60K.DIV.AREA	29/8/16		District Sanitary Inspections. Disinfected Billet 25 occupied by 2/2nd Batt.	
ETRUN			Sprayed (crude oil) Latrines & Midden.	
			" " Yard ground No.3 Billet.	
ST. MICHEL			Withdrew N.C.O. & man from Reinforcement Camp and handed over Books and Materials to 35th Sanitary Section att. to 18th Divn. O.C. Visits D.O.M.S. re St. Michel Camp.	P.S.F.

Medical

Army Form C. 2118

10.

WAR DIARY
or
INTELLIGENCE SUMMARY
(Erase heading not required.)

Instructions regarding War Diaries and Intelligence Summaries are contained in F. S. Regs., Part II. and the Staff Manual respectively. Title Pages will be prepared in manuscript.

Place	Date	Hour	Summary of Events and Information	Remarks and references to Appendices
HERMAVILLE	30/8/16		Made & fixed 5 models for D.A.D.M.S. Arthurs.	
DIV. AREA			District Sanitary Inspection as usual.	MG
TILLOY	31/8/16	6 A.M.	Delivered Transport Lorry to M.T. Supply Column & workshops for Inspection returned at 5 p.m.	
ECOIVRES			District Inspection M.O. 1/4 an. O.C. in charge 1/4 Field Amb. and A Coy 15	MG
HERMAVILLE			Constructing Incinerators and Urinals for outlying Divisional Camps.	

H. S. TEGGIN
Capt.
O.C. SANITARY SECTION
60th (LONDON) DIVISION

MEDICAL.

Vol 4

COMMITTEE FOR THE
MEDICAL HISTORY OF THE WAR
Date   26 OCT 1916

Confidential

War Diary
of
SANITARY SECTION
60th (LONDON) DIVISION

from 1st September 1916
to 30th September 1916

Volume X.

Sept 1916

Medical

Army Form C. 2118

WAR DIARY
or
INTELLIGENCE SUMMARY

SANITARY SECTION
60th (LONDON) DIVISION

(Erase heading not required.)

Instructions regarding War Diaries and Intelligence Summaries are contained in F.S. Regs., Part II. and the Staff Manual respectively. Title Pages will be prepared in manuscript.

No. 1

Place	Date	Hour	Summary of Events and Information	Remarks and references to Appendices
60th Divl AREA	1/9/16		Daily District Inspections.	
MARŒUIL			C.O. visited Town Mayor and inspected District.	
HERMAVILLE			Fitted up Barn at Billet 98 as small workshop for Section. Made and fixed trough Urinal at R.A. H.Q. (Officers) do do Grenade School Camp (Officers) Repaired Grenade School Latrines. Dug fresh incinerator pit at Billet 73 (Reinforcements).	H. Tassart
ETRUN	2/9/16		C.O. visited Town Mayor and inspected District	
HERMAVILLE			Cleaning roads and Billets with fatigue party. Dug Incinerator Pit at R.E. Signals Camp. Disinfections :- Divisional Post Office. Postal Staff Billet. H.Q. Batmens Billet.	H. Tassart
HERMAVILLE	3/9/16		Continued preparation of District Sanitary Area Plans. Made and fixed Urinal at Billet 49. (R.E.)	H. Tassart
Divl AREA	4/9/16		District Sanitary Inspections.	H.S. Tassart

Army Form C. 2118

WAR DIARY or INTELLIGENCE SUMMARY

(Erase heading not required.)

SANITARY SECTION 60th (LONDON) DIVISION

Place	Date	Hour	Summary of Events and Information	Remarks and references to Appendices
HERMAVILLE	4/9/16		Buried dead horse at Billet 22. (M.M.P.)	
			Cleaned up site of Physical Training Camp filling in Latrines & Pits.	
			Sanitary Works:—	
			Made & fixed rough Urinals at Billet 15. R.A.H.Q. (Mens)	
			do. do. Chateau Mens Billet	
			do. do. Billet 79. H.Q. Garage.	
			Made & fixed incinerators at Billet 75. R.A.H.Q.	
BRAY			do do D.A.C. Camp.	
LARASSET			do do Billet 5. B/301.	
ECOIVRES			do do 179th Bgd H.Q., Billet 14.	
Mt. St ELOY			do do 180th Bgde Guard, Billet 5.	
			do Trough Urinal	Ntd To 60th
			do Ablution Trough	
FREVIN CAPELLE			do 6 Grease traps H.Q. of D.A.C.	
DIVL AREA	5/9/16		District Sanitary Inspections	
			C.O. with D.A.D.M.S. 3rd Army 16" inspect. Troops Augous Herche /Ntd To 60th	
			all day	

Medical

Army Form C. 2118

WAR DIARY
or
INTELLIGENCE SUMMARY
SANITARY SECTION
60th (LONDON) DIVISION

(Erase heading not required.)

Instructions regarding War Diaries and Intelligence Summaries are contained in F.S. Regs., Part II. and the Staff Manual respectively. Title Pages will be prepared in manuscript.

3

Place	Date	Hour	Summary of Events and Information	Remarks and references to Appendices
HERMAVILLE	5/9/16		Continued Divisional Sanitary District Plans. Making Sanitary fittings.	
ETRUN			Disinfected by Creosol Spray Nos 25 & 27 Rue de Lemaire.	1st Lieut
DIV. AREA	6/9/16	p.m.	District Sanitary Inspections.	
BRAY			C.O. visited & inspected billets.	
HERMAVILLE			Scavenged billets and Roads. Prepared materials for Sanitary fittings.	
ECOIVRES			Disinfected by Creosol Spray :— H.Q. 179th Hyde Billet to Ryde Field P.O. to Armourers Room at Billet 52.	1st Lieut
ETRUN			Paraffin Sprayed yard of Billet No 3.	
DIV. AREA	7/9/16		District Sanitary Inspections.	
LARASSET		a.m.	C.O. inspected R.F.A. Camps & Billets.	
HERMAVILLE		a.m.	Cleaned Roads.	1st Lieut
HAUTE AVESNES		a.m.	Tried and worked portable Disinfector at Con: Camp for P.A.D.M.S. Lecture. Made models for Sanitary Exhibition. Men C.O. inspected 2/5 2/6 Field Ambulance billets.	

1875 Wt. W593/826 1,000,000 4/15 J.B.C. & A. A.D.S.S./Forms/C. 2118.

Medical

WAR DIARY or INTELLIGENCE SUMMARY

Army Form C. 2118

SANITARY SECTION — 60th (LONDON) DIVISION

4.

(Erase heading not required.)

Instructions regarding War Diaries and Intelligence Summaries are contained in F.S. Regs., Part II. and the Staff Manual respectively. Title Pages will be prepared in manuscript.

Place	Date	Hour	Summary of Events and Information	Remarks and references to Appendices
ECOIVRES	7/9/16		Disinfected Cookhouse and Stables at H.Q. 179th Byde.	
BRAY			Sprayed with crude oil fly breeding areas at Billets 8; 12; 15; 19; and 20. Also 2/14th Batn. Transport Manure Dumps.	18 to 20 ans
ETRUN			Disinfected Officers Mess in RUE du VISANS.	
DIVL. AREA	8/9/16		District Sanitary Inspections.	
MAROEUIL			C.O. in morning to inspect billets & interview Town Major.	
FREVIN CAPELLE			C.O. in afternoon to advise on sanitary condition of LENET FARM.	
HERMAVILLE			Removed latrines from RUE D'IZEL. Made Models for Exhibition area.	No to 05 ans
ECOIVRES			Disinfected N.C.O.s & Mens Bathhouse.	
			Made Biscuit Box Latrine sent for 2/17th Batn. #Q.M.	
LARASSET			Disinfected by Cresol Spray A/302 Cookhouse	
			" " " C/301 do	
			" " " B/301 do	
HERMAVILLE	9/9/16		Scavenged Billets & Inspect Roads	No to 05 ans
			Prepared sketch of Improvised Portable Disinfector for R.A.M.S.	
			Made Exhibition Models.	
			Inspected allergies Helmets and goggles	

Medical

Army Form C. 2118

WAR DIARY
or
INTELLIGENCE SUMMARY

(Erase heading not required.)

SANITARY SECTION
60th (LONDON) DIVISION

No. 5

Instructions regarding War Diaries and Intelligence Summaries are contained in F.S. Regs., Part II. and the Staff Manual respectively. Title Pages will be prepared in manuscript.

Place	Date	Hour	Summary of Events and Information	Remarks and references to Appendices
HERMAVILLE	10/9/16		Built stone Incinerator at Billet 98. (San. Sec.)	1st Sept
			Made and fixed 2 Rough Urinals at C.R.E.H.Q. Dug new pits and removed and repaired existing Latrine Seats	
FREVIN CAPPELLE	11/9/16		C.O. inspect Billets & Camps occupied by D.A.C	
ECOIVRES			Made and delivered to TOWN MAJOR 5 Biscuit Box Latrine Seats	
HERMAVILLE			Made copy of washing plan of D.A.D.M.S. Improvised Portable Disinfector	1st Sept
			Made and fixed Rough Urinals at No.4 H.Q. Officers' Mess Billet 27. M.P. Billet	
			do do Exhibition Models	
			N.C.O. and Fatigue Party cleaning roads.	
DIV. AREA	12/9/16		District Sanitary Inspections.	
HAUTES AVESNES			do do	1st Sept
FREVIN CAPPELLE			Made & fixed Iron Incinerator for Entrenching Batts.	
ECOIVRES			do do	
			Disinfected by Cresol Spray Officers Baths Billet 22. (Frévin)	
			Made out delivered to 2/17th Batt. Q.M. 4 Latrine Box Seats	
			O.C. inspects premises where men & butter are sold to the troops	

1875 Wt. W593/826 1,000,000 4/15 J.B.C. & A. A.D.S.S./Forms/C. 2118.

Medical

Army Form C. 2118

WAR DIARY
or
INTELLIGENCE SUMMARY
(Erase heading not required.)

SANITARY SECTION
60th (LONDON) DIVISION

6

Instructions regarding War Diaries and Intelligence Summaries are contained in F.S. Regs., Part II. and the Staff Manual respectively. Title Pages will be prepared in manuscript.

Place	Date	Hour	Summary of Events and Information	Remarks and references to Appendices
HERMAVILLE	12/9/16		Roofed and covered H.Q. Garage Latrine. Made and fixed new troughs & urinal at No. 3 Officers' Mess.	Attached
BRAY			San. Sec. N.C.O. and fatigue party cleared streets. Disinfected by Creol Spray. Billet 14.	
DIV. AREA	13/9/16		District Sanitary Inspections.	
LARASSET			C.O. inspected R.F.A. Camps and Lines and Staff Captain R.A. C.O. to ~~P.M.~~ ~~LILLERS~~ 3 m/t D.A.D.M.S. to meet D.M.S. 1st Army	Attached
ECOIVRES			Sprayed with crude oil midden at Billet 75.	
MAROEUIL			Made & fixed 2 trough urinals for O.C. Salvage Coy.	
HERMAVILLE			Cleaned and rearranged roads with fatigue party of 7.	
DIV. AREA	14/9/16	a.m.	C.O. visited FREVIN CAPPELLE and A.C.C. to inspect D.A.C. and R.F.A. Camps and HAUTE AVESNES and MAROEUIL to inspect Billets. District Sanitary Inspections.	Attached
BRAY			Made & fixed pub incinerator for M.G.C. Transport at Billet 19. Disinfected by Creol Spray. Billets 4 & 25.	
MT. ST. ELOY			do	Officers Quarters, Mess & Kitchen 2 Cookhouses D.M. Store & Sgts Mess and Billet No. 5. all 301 B. R.F.A.
LARASSET			do	

Madras

Army Form C. 2118

WAR DIARY
or
INTELLIGENCE SUMMARY — SANITARY SECTION
60th (LONDON) DIVISION

(Erase heading not required.)

Instructions regarding War Diaries and Intelligence Summaries are contained in F.S. Regs., Part II. and the Staff Manual respectively. Title Pages will be prepared in manuscript.

Place	Date	Hour	Summary of Events and Information	Remarks and references to Appendices
DIV. AREA	15/9/16		District Sanitary Inspection	
HAUTES AVESNES		a.m	C.O. visited Transport Lines 181st Bde. ACQ to inspect Ecouires to inspect premises rending near Butter	
		afternoon	HAUTE AYESNES to inspect Div Train Camps. LEMET FARM R 3A 2no	
BRAY			Made and fixed Bor Seat Latrine at Billet 19.	It J. Tolbert
HERMAVILLE			do Trough Urinal at Billet adjoining 118.	
			Made Models for Exhibition	
HAUTES AVESNES	16/9/16	a.m	Made and fixed Memo covered Latrine + Urinal at Divl. Theatre O.C. was and inspect work in progress	Hd Tolbert
HERMAVILLE			Continued making Exhibition Models Scavenged and Cleaned Yards	
HERMAVILLE	17/9/16		Cleaned up Billet 98. and Limewashed cookhouse Repaired Latrine at Billet 95.	It J. Tolbert
			Made models for Exhibition Repaired made of stove at Billet 92.	

1875 Wt. W593/826 1,000,000 4/15 J.B.C. & A. A.D.S.S./Forms/C. 2118.

Medical

Army Form C. 2118

WAR DIARY
or
INTELLIGENCE SUMMARY
(Erase heading not required.)

SANITARY SECTION
60th (LONDON) DIVISION

8

Instructions regarding War Diaries and Intelligence Summaries are contained in F.S. Regs., Part II. and the Staff Manual respectively. Title Pages will be prepared in manuscript.

Place	Date	Hour	Summary of Events and Information	Remarks and references to Appendices
DIVL AREA	18/9/16		District Sanitary Inspections.	
HERMAVILLE			Continued making models for Exhibition. Sprayed with crude oil stagnant water etc of Billet 22.	Note own
DIVL AREA	19/9/16		District Sanitary Inspections.	
MT. ST. ELOY			C.O. inspected Gun emplacement of D/303, which was disinfected by Cresol Spray.	
ECOIVRES			C.O. visited billets	H/3 to OSA
HERMAVILLE			Drew from A.O.D. and issued to Personnel of Section 27 Helmets Steeland 28 Helmets anti-gas P.H.G. (Received from T.F. Depot Medical Unit) Chelsea. Received and issued to men gifts (tobacco) from T.F. Depot Medical Unit to CHELSEA. Constructed models for Exhibition.	
HERMAVILLE	20/9/16		Continued Models for Exhibition. Returned to A.O.D. Surplus P.H. Anti-gas Helmets No 27. Inspected all Anti-gas Helmets of Personnel.	Note own
LILLERS			C.O. attended conference of Sanitary Officers convened by D.M.S. 1st Army all day.	
HERMAVILLE	21/9/16		G.O.C. Divn. inspected Exhibition of Sanitary Models and Latrin Workshop. Scavenged Roads and cleaned ditches with fatigue party of 8 men. Delivered to french R.y Dump 1 ablution Bench & 1 Latrine Box seat for Don 303 Battery	H/S Tabbr

1875 Wt. W593/826 1,000,000 4/15 J.B.C. & A. A.D.S.S./Forms/C.2118.

Medical

Army Form C. 2118

WAR DIARY
or
INTELLIGENCE SUMMARY
(Erase heading not required.)

SANITARY SECTION
60th (LONDON) DIVISION

Place	Date	Hour	Summary of Events and Information	Remarks and references to Appendices
HERMAVILLE	22/9/16		Erected at Exhibition Area all completed Models of Field Sanitary Appliances	Note 85m.
		2-30 p.m.	D.M.S. 1st Army inspected Exhibition Area, Billet and Workshops. Drew Blankets from A.O.D. and issued 1 each to Personnel and men attached (28)	
HERMAVILLE	23/9/16	9 a.m.	Transport Lorry to M.T. Depot for periodical inspection returning at 5 p.m. Made and fixed Rough Urinals at Billet 110 Signal Coy (Officers) do 110 do (Men) do 27 Postal Clerks (Men) Fitted new latrine seat at Billet 98.	Note 83m.
		12 midday	C.O. with A.D.M.S. visited 61st Divisional Sanitary Section Workshops. Lozenger Roads.	
LA GORQUE				
HERMAVILLE	24/9/16	9 a.m.	Pte/2 174864 Pte-W.B. Beeston A.S.C. (M.T.) reported with Ford Motor Ambulance T/24577 from 25th Ambulance for duty. Worked at further Sanitary Models. Cleared roads and scavenged Billets.	Note 82m.

Medical

Army Form C. 2118

WAR DIARY
or
INTELLIGENCE SUMMARY
(Erase heading not required.)

SANITARY SECTION
60th (LONDON) DIVISION

10.

Instructions regarding War Diaries and Intelligence Summaries are contained in F.S. Regs., Part II, and the Staff Manual respectively. Title Pages will be prepared in manuscript.

Place	Date	Hour	Summary of Events and Information	Remarks and references to Appendices
DIV AREA	23/9/16		District Sanitary Inspections and Inspection of Divisional Bath Cents.	
BRAY, ECOIVRES HERMAVILLE			C.O. visited "Break" and Rest Camp. Worked at Public Latrine in Rue DIZEL. Returned to A.O.D. 25 Lum Curtains and 1 Eye Sponge.	Photograph
HAUTES AVESNES			Made and fixed Covered Latrine and Urinal at Divisional Theatre.	
ECOIVRES			Made and delivered to 2/17th Batn. 2730x Latrine seats.	
DIV AREA	24/9/16		C.O. to BRAY & to ECOIVRES & MT. ST. ELOIS } to make "Break" and Rest Camps.	
HERMAVILLE			District Sanitary Inspections. Disinfected by Cresol Spray Billet 21. do 114.	Photograph
LARASSET			Whitewashed kitchen at No 4 H.Q. Mess Garage with conde oz A.P.M.'s Stable yard.	
ECOIVRES			Disinfected Cookhouse and Mess of 301st Bgde R.F.A. do By Cresol spray Billets 18, 22, & 52 and Officers Bath house.	
MAROEUIL			Carted to Baths for A.O.D. 8 sacks of Mens worn Clothing.	

1875 Wt. W593/826 1,000,000 4/15 J.B.C. & A. A.D.S.S./Forms/C. 2118.

Medical

Army Form C. 2118

WAR DIARY
or
INTELLIGENCE SUMMARY — SANITARY SECTION
60th (LONDON) DIVISION

(Erase heading not required.)

Instructions regarding War Diaries and Intelligence Summaries are contained in F.S. Regs., Part II. and the Staff Manual respectively. Title Pages will be prepared in manuscript.

11

Place	Date	Hour	Summary of Events and Information	Remarks and references to Appendices
DIVL AREA	27/9/16		District and Water Cart Inspection.	
A.C.O. FREVIN CAPELLE			C.O. inspected. D.A.O. Lines and R.F.A. Lines	
FREVIN CAPELLE			Made + fixed Iron Incinerator for No.2 Section of Entrenching Coy.	MS Taton
LARASSET			Disinfected by Cresol Spray all Cookhouses of 301 + 302 Brigades of R.F.A.	
ETRUN			do — Billet 27. 2/21st Battn Flares.	
			do — do 19 3/24th to	
DIVL AREA	28/9/16		District and Water Cart Inspection.	
			C.O. to MAROEUIL to interview Town Major and	
			to ETRUN } inspected Billets	MF Tirson
HERMAVILLE			Completed covered Latrine + Urinal (for Men) in RUE D'IZEL	
			Scavenged Roads	
HAUTES AVESNES			Made + fixed Iron Incinerator for No. 4 Coy A.S.C.	
ECOIVRES			Made + delivered to Town Major 2 Rosa Latrine tents.	
			O.C. 2/4th Field Ambulance 1 do	

Medical.

Army Form C. 2118

WAR DIARY or INTELLIGENCE SUMMARY

(Erase heading not required.)

SANITARY SECTION
60th (LONDON) DIVISION

Instructions regarding War Diaries and Intelligence Summaries are contained in F.S. Regs., Part II. and the Staff Manual respectively. Title Pages will be prepared in manuscript.

Place	Date	Hour	Summary of Events and Information	Remarks and references to Appendices
DIV AREA	29/9/16		District & Water Cart Inspections.	12
BRAY			C.O. to MAROEUIL to inspect billets	
Mt. St. ELOY			Work fatigue party damaged roads & billets.	
			Made & fixed 300 latrine seats at 180 hrs to Police Billet	
ETRUN			Evacuated Pvt. No. 2 of 2/20th Battn of suspected Diphtheria case	to Hosp.
			No. 27 Rue BENFERT.	
HERMAVILLE			Billet 65. (Reinforcements)	
			Cleaned Roads & Ditches	
			Made latrine boards for Inhabited area	
ECOIVRES			Made & delivered specimen Wire Latrine seats to 2/17th Batta 2.	
MAROEUIL			2/15 to 1	
			Disinfected dug-outs by British Cemetery	
HERMAVILLE	30/9/16		Completed Sketch Plans of Sanitary Districts	
			Made 7 – 60th Pattern Urinals	
			Commenced work on Chlorination Filter Boxes for Convalescent Camp Baths	
			Made framework for shelter for O.D. Aeration trench	He Tebb A.
			Scavenged Roads and Billets	

H. S. Tebb A.
Capt.
O/C SANITARY SECTION
60th (LONDON) DIVISION

1875 Wt. W593/826 1,000,000 4/15 J.B.C. & A. A.D.S.S./Forms/C.2118.

66th Div. Sanitection

Cough.

COMMITTEE FOR THE
MEDICAL HISTORY OF THE WAR
Date -2 DEC. 1916

Vol 5

Confidential

War Diary
of

SANITARY SECTION
60th (LONDON DIVISION)

from 1st October 1916
to 31st October 1916

Sheets 1 to 11

WAR DIARY
INTELLIGENCE SUMMARY

Army Form C. 2118

SANITARY SECTION
60th (LONDON) DIVISION

Place	Date	Hour	Summary of Events and Information	Remarks and references to Appendices
HERMAVILLE	1/10/16		District Sanitary Inspection. Prepared Notice Boards for Sanitary Inspection. Worked at Chlorinator, Latrine Boxes for Div. Camp. Bath house waste water.	H.T.
HERMAVILLE	2/10/16		District Sanitary Inspections of Divisional Area. Made waste pipes for 179th & 15pdr Albuton Branch. Prepared Boxes for Box seat Latrines.	
FREVIN CAPELLE			Scavenged Camps & Worked on Entrenching Coy. Bivouac Camp and Woolooh. Made & fixed 2 Box seat Latrine tops for M.G.C. Transport of 179th Bgde.	yes
BRAY				
ECOIVRES			Made & delivered to Town Major 2 Box Latrine seats, 160th Jantim kernel. do do to Priest at Billet 68. 1 Box Latrine seat.	
HAUTES AVESNES			Disinfected by Cresol Spray orderly Room of XVII Corps Syllabits (suspected Diphtheria). do do Billet No 13, Kitchen to Divl Train Officers Mess. } H.Q. do do do 18. Guard room Divl Train } Coy. do do do Huts 8 & 8A of Divn. Train.	
Mt. ST. ELOI			O.C. awaits & majors Rest Camp 180 Bde	
HERMAVILLE	3/10/16		District Sanitary Inspection of Divl Area. Worked at Conv. Camps Bath house Rea filters. Scavenged Roads & Billets.	yes
Mt. ST. ELOI			Made & delivered Specimen Box seat for Latrines to Staff Capt. 180 & 181 Bde.	

Manuals

Army Form C. 2118

WAR DIARY
or
INTELLIGENCE SUMMARY

SANITARY SECTION
60th (LONDON) DIVISION

(Erase heading not required.)

Instructions regarding War Diaries and Intelligence Summaries are contained in F.S. Regs., Part II. and the Staff Manual respectively. Title Pages will be prepared in manuscript.

2.

Place	Date	Hour	Summary of Events and Information	Remarks and references to Appendices
FREVIN CAPELLE	3/10/16		Made & delivered 1 iron incinerator to D.A.C.	
HAUTES AVESNES			do 1 to Town Major	Nil
			Disinfected by Creole Spray:- Billet No.13. Town Majors' Office do 17,18, & 21. H.Q. Coy. Divl. Train. do 21. 2/6th 2 Field Ambulance	
ETRUN			O.C. visits and inspects drainage at 181st Bde. H.Q. morning afterno	
HERMAVILLE	4/10/16		District Sanitary Inspection of Divl. Area Scavenged Roads Worked at Cor. Camp Bath-house filter Painted notices for Inhalation Models. O.C. inspects mobile Vet. Section Camp.	Nil
AUBIGNY ETRUN			O.C. visits sanitary work in operation at 181st Bde HQ	
HERMAVILLE	5/10/16		District sanitary & Water Cart Inspections. Scavenged & swept Roads. Engraving notices for Inhalation Models. Worked at Sanitary Appliances.	Nil
MARŒUIL ETRUN ECOIVRES			O.C. visits inspects Billets	

1875 Wt W593/826 1,000,000 4/15 J.B.C. & A. A.D.S.S./Forms/C. 2118.

Material

Army Form C. 2118

WAR DIARY
or
INTELLIGENCE SUMMARY
(Erase heading not required.)

SANITARY SECTION
60th (LONDON) DIVISION

3

Instructions regarding War Diaries and Intelligence Summaries are contained in F. S. Regs., Part II. and the Staff Manual respectively. Title Pages will be prepared in manuscript.

Place	Date	Hour	Summary of Events and Information	Remarks and references to Appendices
HERMAVILLE	6/10/16		District Sanitary & Hut Cart Inspections.	
MT. ST. ELOY			Lavengel & Suspect Roads	
ETRUN			Disinfector Dug out of PON 303. after Spotted Fever.	
BRAY			No. 29 Rue BENFERT Disinfected. Crest Spayed :- Billet 20. Manure in yard & pigstye	
			" 21. do to	NGT
			" 22. Cookhouse	
			" 18. 2 m. Store of 2/13th & all 2/13 Hsatrines	
			" 7. Ambulance Street	
MARDEVIL			2" dry onto in South Street	
			Spayed with Crude Oil Manure heaps at Nos 1, 2, 9, 11, 12, 15, 19, 25, & 27 Amyen Road.	
			do do No. 1 Ambulance Street	
ACQ CAPELLE FERMONT			OC visits Inspects R.F.A. Camps "Tilloy"	
HERMAVILLE	7/10/16		Lavenged Roads & Billets	
			Disinfecting notes for Prohibition Models.	
AUBIGNY			Multiplied	
			Roofed & Screened 1 cent Officers' Latrine with Urinal for Mob. Vet. Sector.	NGT
HAUTES AVESNES			" 2 seat Mens do	
MARDEUIL			Urinal No. 2. A.S.C. Refilling Camp Latrines.	
ETRUN			OC. Inspects Billets	

1875 Wt. W593/826 1,000,000 4/15 J.B.C. & A. A.D.S.S./Forms/C. 2118.

Manuel

Army Form C. 2118

WAR DIARY
or
INTELLIGENCE SUMMARY

SANITARY SECTION
60th (LONDON) DIVISION

4.

(Erase heading not required.)

Instructions regarding War Diaries and Intelligence Summaries are contained in F. S. Regs., Part II and the Staff Manual respectively. Title Pages will be prepared in manuscript.

Place	Date	Hour	Summary of Events and Information	Remarks and references to Appendices
HERMAVILLE	8/10/16		Worked generally at Sanitary Appliances.	
AUBIGNY			Made and fixed Complete Camel Cookhouse & Mobile Veterinary Section. 1 Night Urinal	Not
HERMAVILLE	9/10/16		District Sanitary & Latrine Cart Inspections. Surveyed Roads. Sanitary Appliances made & fixed	
ECOIVRES			5 Box Latrine seats H.Q. 179th Byde.	
			1 Iron Incinerator 2/17th Battn.	
			1 do do Transport.	
MT. ST. ELOY			1 Urinal at Billet 23.	Nat
FREVIN CAPPELLE			1 Urinal at Anti-gas School — 1 Urinal at D.A.C. Section 2.	
CAPPELLE FERMONT			1 Iron Incinerator }	
			5 Box Latrine Seats } 303 Byde of R.F.A.	
			1 Grease trap }	
			4 Urinals }	
BRAY			1 Box Latrine seat 179th Byde M.G.C.	
A.C.Q.			1 Iron Incinerator } 21st Reserve A.S.C.	
			1 Grease trap }	
ECOIVRES	am		1 Iron Incinerator C Battery 303 Byde R.F.A.	
HAUTE AVESNES	pm		O.C. inspects Camp Orders	

1875 Wt. W593/826 1,000,000 4/15 J.B.C. & A. A.D.S.S./Forms/C. 2118.

Marini

Army Form C. 2118

5.

WAR DIARY
~~INTELLIGENCE SUMMARY~~

SANITARY SECTION
60th (LONDON) DIVISION

(Erase heading not required.)

Instructions regarding War Diaries and Intelligence Summaries are contained in F. S. Regs., Part II. and the Staff Manual respectively. Title Pages will be prepared in manuscript.

Place	Date	Hour	Summary of Events and Information	Remarks and references to Appendices
LARESSET.	9/10/16		Sanitary Appliances Made & Fixed. 3 Boo Latrine seats } to D Battery 303 Bgde R.F.A. 1 Urinal 3 Ablution Bench Trippos } 301 & 302 Bgdes. 4 Urinals } 301 Howitzer Bgde 5 Urinals } A.S.C. Divl. Train. 1 Grease Trap }	MT
HAUTES AVESNES.				
HERMAVILLE	10/10/16	11 a.m.	District Sanitary Inspection. Surveyed Roads & Billets. Motor Lorry to A.S.C. M.T. for Inspection Worked at Corr. Camps Bath house Filter Boxes. Painted Exhibition Models	sat
HAUTES AVESNES			Sprayed :- Town Majors Office Barn at No 3. Billet	
ECOURES MARŒUIL HAUTE AVESNES	3 a.m 3 pm		O.C. inspected Camps Carts Billets.	
HERMAVILLE	11/10/16		Painted Exhibition Models. Constructed Sanitary Appliances. Surveyed Roads & Billets.	VoT

Manual

WAR DIARY
INTELLIGENCE SUMMARY
(Erase heading not required.)

SANITARY SECTION
60th (LONDON) DIVISION

Army Form C. 2118

6.

Place	Date	Hour	Summary of Events and Information	Remarks and references to Appendices
HERMAVILLE	12/10/16		District Sanitary Inspections.	
			Made at Exhibition Area supporting (greens) "trench fires".	
ETRUN			Swept Roads	
AUBIGNY			Disinfected Orangery at Billet 77.	
			Made + fixed at H.Q. 181st R.F.A. Officers' 2 seat Box Latrine + Urinal.	1 ost
HAUTES AVESNES			do 1 Iron Incinerator for M. of. Vet. Section	
MAROEUIL			do 1 do 2/6th L. Field Amber.	
ETRUN			do 1 do A.S.C. Train	
			Sprayed Manure at Nos 13, 15, + 17 Ambulance Horse Belle 6.	
			O.C. inspected.	
HERMAVILLE	13/10/16		District Sanitary Inspections.	
ACQ			Disinfected Billet No. 87. (inspected O.S.M.)	
HERMAVILLE			Made duplicates of Exhibition Models for 3rd Army.	180
			Painted Original and Exhibition Sanitary Models.	
			Made + fixed complete covered Latrine at Billet 71.	
			Continued work on Con. Camp Nutt House filter.	
MT. ST ELOI ECOIVRES			O.C. inspected Camps "Trollers"	

Medical

Army Form C. 2118

WAR DIARY
—or—
INTELLIGENCE SUMMARY

SANITARY SECTION
60th (LONDON) DIVISION

(Erase heading not required.)

Instructions regarding War Diaries and Intelligence Summaries are contained in F.S. Regs., Part II. and the Staff Manual respectively. Title Pages will be prepared in manuscript.

Place	Date	Hour	Summary of Events and Information	Remarks and references to Appendices
HERMAVILLE	14/10/16		District Sanitary Inspections. Tried 2 precipitation boxes at Corps Camp Bathhouse. Made Chlorate Models for 3rd Army.	7.
HAUTES AVESNES			Rots inspected. 3 Latrine Boxes sent for 2/6 at London Field Ambulance.	Yes
AUBIGNY FERFAY CAPELLE			1 Complete nozzle offices latrine with urinal – H.Q. Coy. Divl. Train	
			On inspected R.F.A. Camp & Mobile Vet. Section Camp	
HERMAVILLE	15/10/16	2.40 p.m.	Exhibition Area inspected by I.A.D.M.S. 1st Army	Yes
			Contd. duplicate Models for 3rd Army. Typewriting for Exhibition Area.	
HERMAVILLE	16/10/16		District Sanitary Inspections, and Funds at H.Q. Lovencourt. Sanitary Appliances made & fixed :–	Yes
ECOIVRES			2 Grease Traps 179th Fg.Ale 3 Latrine Buckets 2/19th Transport 3 Refuse Bags Civil Billets 1 Iron Incinerator 2/4th L. Field Ambce.	
FREVIN CAPPELLE			2 Incinerators, 3 Latrine Boxes sents, 3 urinals. to D.A.C. 4 Refuse Bags to Divl. Train Corps (1 each)	
HAUTES AVESNES				
ETRUN MAROEUIL			Farmers Bathhouse with cresol inspected Billets.	

Medical

Army Form C. 2118

WAR DIARY
or
INTELLIGENCE SUMMARY

SANITARY SECTION
60th (LONDON) DIVISION

8.

(Erase heading not required.)

Instructions regarding War Diaries and Intelligence Summaries are contained in F.S. Regs., Part II. and the Staff Manual respectively. Title Pages will be prepared in manuscript.

Place	Date	Hour	Summary of Events and Information	Remarks and references to Appendices
HERMAVILLE	17/10/16		District Sanitary Inspections.	
BRAY			Conveyed Billets with fatigue parties.	
AUBIGNY			Modified Aldershot Bench & Grease trap for Mobile Veterinary Section.	JFOT
EBOIVRES			O.C. No. 5 150 Bde Transport Train. C.R.E.	
HERMAVILLE	18/9/16		District Sanitary Inspections.	
			Conveyed and put roads.	
			Made duplicate Models for 3rd Army	
ECOIVRES			Made & delivered to Town Major	
Mt ST ELOY			5 Urinals, 2 Incinerators, 18 Latrine Seats	
ACQ			180th Bgde	5 13mo seats for Latrines	
BRAY			303 Bgde RFA 6 do	
FREVENT			Disinfected (2/14th) quarter occupied by suspected case of Measles.	14—
			Sent to report REVENT for billeting accommodation of Village	
HERMAVILLE	19/10/16		No. 737. Acting Lloyd Howard F. granted one months leave under G.R.O. 1679.	JFOT
			Painted duplicate Models for 3rd Army.	
			Removed original Disinfector Models from Cm Camp handed in Lorry.	
			Worked at Cm Camp Bath House Bone Gutter.	
LA COUROY			Arranged Billets for Divisional HQ Troops.	
HERMAVILLE	20/10/16		No. 737. Acting Lloyd Howard F. Left on months leave to England.	JFOT
LILLERS			Delivered by Lorry 37 Exhibition Sanitary Models to D.A.D.M.S. 1st Army O.C accompanied	

1875 Wt. W593/826 1,000,000 4/15 J.B.C. & A. A.D.S.S./Forms/C. 2118.

Manual

Army Form C. 2118

WAR DIARY
SANITARY SECTION 60th (LONDON) DIVISION
INTELLIGENCE SUMMARY
(Erase heading not required.)

Instructions regarding War Diaries and Intelligence Summaries are contained in F.S. Regs., Part II and the Staff Manual respectively. Title Pages will be prepared in manuscript.

9

Place	Date	Hour	Summary of Events and Information	Remarks and references to Appendices
HERMAVILLE	21/10/16		Completed & painted duplicate Models for 3rd Army. Models at Con. Camp Bath house filter.	Nil
ECOIVRES MAROEUIL			Made Sanitary appliances pending a move from the District. O.C. Inspected billets	Nil
HERMAVILLE	22/10/16		Made Sanitary appliances. Prepared notice for duplicate Models	Nil
HERMAVILLE	23/10/16		Prepared to move with H.Q. to new District. FODEN-THRESH Disinfector taken in charge. M/2/101228 Lcpl. Sanderson L.H. } A.S.C.M.T. take on strength for billeting substituted M/2/100683 Pte. Kirby J.A. } C.O. Inspected billets with Camp Commandant.	
LE COURY			delivered 13 duplicate exhibition Models to D.A.D.M.S. 3rd Army.	Nil
ST. POL				
HERMAVILLE	24/10/16	9-30 A.M.	Left with lorry + advance party for LECOURAY.	
LECOURAY		10-30 A.M.	Installed advance party and part of Stores at Billet 78. Recalled at 11-30 a.m. to Hermaville.	
HERMAVILLE		1 P.M.	Returned with party and stores to Billet 78.	160
		4 P.M.	No. 3034 Lcpl. Marsh admitted to Canadian Field Ambulance Hospital O.C. Later O.C. San Section Canadian Division round the works. Duties.	

Medical

Army Form C. 2118

10.

WAR DIARY
— of —
INTELLIGENCE SUMMARY

(Erase heading not required.)

SANITARY SECTION
60th (LONDON) DIVISION

Instructions regarding War Diaries and Intelligence Summaries are contained in F.S. Regs., Part II. and the Staff Manual respectively. Title Pages will be prepared in manuscript.

Place	Date	Hour	Summary of Events and Information	Remarks and references to Appendices
HERMAVILLE	25/10/16	12-50 midday	Moved with advance party and party of stores to	1st
HOUVIN-HOUVIGNEUL		1-50 p.m.	and installed same at Billet 25.	
HERMAVILLE	26/10/16	2 p.m.	Moved A.D.M.S. Office equipment & Staff with remainder of San. Section Stores & Personnel by road to	1st
HOUVIN-HOUVIGNEUL		4 p.m.	and Installed at 24 & 25 Billets respectively.	
HOUVIN-HOUVIGNEUL	27/10/16	2 p.m.	Attended to Sanitation of H.Q. Units Billets. Foden Steel Disinfector reported after activation by A.S.C. M.T. and Car from Dist. by LIENCOURT.	1st
HOUVIN-HOUVIGNEUL	28/10/16	8-30 a.m.	Marched Section by road to	1st
FROHEN-LE-GRANDE		3-15 p.m.	arrived at new Billet Daimler Lorry, Foden Lorry and A.D.M.S. Staff and Section Stores travelling by Road.	
FROHEN-LE-GRANDE	29/10/16	8-30	Marched Section by road to	1st
BERNAVILLE		11 a.m.	arrived at new Billet. Daimler Lorry, Foden Lorry, A.D.M.S. Staff, & Section Stores travelling by road.	

1875. Wt. W593/826 1,000,000 4/15 J.B.C. & A. A.D.S.S./Forms/C 2118.

Army Form C. 2118

WAR DIARY
INTELLIGENCE SUMMARY
(Erase heading not required.)

SANITARY SECTION
60th (LONDON) DIVISION

Instructions regarding War Diaries and Intelligence Summaries are contained in F. S. Regs., Part II. and the Staff Manual respectively. Title Pages will be prepared in manuscript.

Place	Date	Hour	Summary of Events and Information	Remarks and references to Appendices
BERNAVILLE	30/10/16		Allotted Sanitary areas in the Town and arranged for Refuse Collections daily from all billets.	
BERNAVILLE	31/10/16		Supervised Town Scavenging and Refuse Collections.	

W. Tabell
Capt
O.C. Sanitary Section
60th (London) Division

In the Field
1st November 1916.

Medical

CONFIDENTIAL

140/949

Nov 1916

War Diary
of
60th Divisional Sanitary Section

from 1st November 1916 to 30th November 1916. (incl.)

Sheet 1

COMMITTEE FOR THE
MEDICAL HISTORY OF THE WAR
Date 30 APR. 1917

SANITARY SECTION
60th (LONDON DIVISION) Army Form C. 2118.

WAR DIARY
INTELLIGENCE SUMMARY
(Erase heading not required.)

Medical

Sheet 1.

Instructions regarding War Diaries and Intelligence Summaries are contained in F.S. Regs., Part II and the Staff Manual respectively. Title pages will be prepared in manuscript.

Place	Date	Hour	Summary of Events and Information	Remarks and references to Appendices
BERNAVILLE	1/11/16		Inspected Billets and carried out Street & Billet Scavenging	H.S.T.
BERNAVILLE	2/11/16		Continued daily Sanitary Supervision. Packed Lorry with Stores preparatory to moving.	H.S.T.
BERNAVILLE	3/11/16	9-30 AM	Marched out with Transport & Stores and proceeded to —	H.S.T.
AILLY-LE-HAUTE CLOCHER		2 P.M.	Arrived at Billet N.o 12. with Foden Thresh Disinfector AS 290 attached.	
		4 P.M.	Detailed parties to make H.Q. Latrines.	
AILLY-LE-HAUTE CLOCHER	4/11/16		Divided D.H.Q. Village into 4 Areas & commenced Sanitary Supervision.	H.S.T.
AILLY-LE-HAUTE CLOCHER	5/11/16		Daily Sanitary Supervision Continued.	H.S.T.
DIV. AREA			Divided for daily Sanitary Inspection the remainder of Division Area into 11 Districts and commenced daily Inspections.	
AILLY-LE-H-C.	5/11/16		Daily District Supervision Continued. Disinfected by Foden Thresh Disinfector AS 290 29 Blankets 10 articles of Clothing of H.Q. Unit	H.S.T. 65oH

WAR DIARY
INTELLIGENCE SUMMARY

Army Form C. 2118.

SANITARY SECTION
60th (LONDON) DIVISION

Sheet No. 2

Manual

Place	Date	Hour	Summary of Events and Information	Remarks and references to Appendices
AILLY-LE-HAUTE CLOCHER	6/11/16		Daily District Inspection of Divisional Area Cont'd. Disinfected 355 Blankets of 2/19th London Regt.	1st S.T.
AILLY-LE-HAUTE CLOCHER	7/11/16	11 p.m.	Daily District Inspection. Disinfected 332 Blankets of 2/19th London Regt. Leave granted to No. 2790 Staff Sgt. D.M. NEIL } 6-13th December 1916. " " 3061 a/S/S. H.J. FRANKLIN } proceed to ENGLAND.	1st S.T.
AILLY-L-H-C. BUSSUS	8/11/16		District Inspections as usual. Disinfected by Foden Thresh 127 Blankets — 697 other articles for 2/17th Bn.	1st S.T.
AILLY-LE-HAUTE CLOCHER BELLANCOURT	9/11/16		District Inspections as usual. Disinfected by Foden Thresh 892 Blankets 360 other articles for 2/16 Bn.	1st S.T.
AILLY-L-H-C. VAUCHELLES-LES-QUESNOY	10/11/16		District Inspections as usual. Disinfected by Foden Thresh { 869 Blankets for 2/13th Batt'n L.R. 219 do do M.C. Coy 179th.	1st S.T.

WAR DIARY
INTELLIGENCE SUMMARY

SANITARY SECTION
60th (LONDON) DIVISION
Army Form C. 2118.
Sheet No. 3

Medical

Place	Date	Hour	Summary of Events and Information	Remarks and references to Appendices
AILLY-L-H-C.	11/11/16		District Inspections of Divisional Area as usual. No. 3039. Cpl. S.H. BLACKABY (unpaid) granted Special Leave to proceed to ENGLAND from 11/11/16 – 16th instants.	NST
BUCNY L'ABBE			Disinfected by Foden Thresh 880 Blankets for 2/14th Battn. L.R.	
AILLY-L-H-C.	12/11/16		District Inspections as usual.	
BUCNY L'ABBE			Disinfected by Foden Thresh { 681 Blankets for 2/15th Battn. L.R. 50 do 2/4th Field Ambce. 208 do No.2. Coy Divl Train.	NST
AILLY-L-H-C.	13/11/16		District Inspection as usual.	
EAUCOURT			Disinfected by Foden Thresh 621 Blankets for 2/4th Field Ambce.	NST
AILLY-L-H-C.	14/11/16		District as usual. M2 180959 Driver GREENDALE & M2 3108 Driver Lumber, G. with Foden Thresh Lorry No. T 5348 Reported from Corps H.Q. to assist with Divisional Unit Disinfections.	NST
EAUCOURT			Disinfected by T 348 300 Blankets of 2/19th Battn. L.R. do T 290 263 do 2/4th R.E.	

A.5834 Wt. W4973/M687 750,000 8/16 D. D. & L. Ltd. Forms/C.2118/13.

WAR DIARY

SANITARY SECTION
60th (LONDON) DIVISION

Army Form C. 2118.

INTELLIGENCE SUMMARY.
(Erase heading not required)

No. 7. Sheet

Medical

Instructions regarding War Diaries and Intelligence Summaries are contained in F.S. Regs., Part II. and the Staff Manual respectively. Title pages will be prepared in manuscript.

Place	Date	Hour	Summary of Events and Information	Remarks and references to Appendices
AILLY-LE-HAUT-CLOCHER	15/11/16		Latrines as usual. Foden Wheel Disinfector ↑ S290 Broken down. Portable Thresh from 35th C.C.S. Disinfected	N&T 36M
BRUCAMPS			S290 Repaired & Disinfected 50 Blankets for 181st T.M. Batty 184. do. 181st M.G. Coy.	
AILLY-L-H-C.		9pm	2790 S/Sgt P.M. NEIL & 3061 2/Sgt H.T. FRANKLIN reported off leave having road disembused from 13th to 15th instants owing to travelling delays. 88631 Pte Adamson J.B. 907 Blankets Disinfected 907 Blankets for 2/62nd Battn of L.R. 66369 Pte Bowler L., & 88646 Pte Atherley A.H. reported to complete establishment Part XII.	
AILLY-L-H-C	16/11/16		District Inspections as usual.	
BRUCAMPS			F-THRESH Disinfected 1200 water bottles for 2/22nd Battn of L.R. ↑ S290 do. 870 Blankets " 2/23rd do. do. ↑ S290 do. 250 do. do. 180 M.G. Coy.	H-85"
ERGNIES				
CORENFLOS			↑ S348 do. 800 do. do. 2/174 Battn of L.R.	
AILLY-LE-HAUT-CLOCHER	17/11/16	9pm	District Inspection as usual. Two from A.O.D. find overzero equipment. No. 3039 Cpl S.H. Beazley reported off leave having been granted on extension owing to delay in travelling.	H-7.
BUSSUS			↑ S348 Disinfected 300 Blankets for 2/6th R.E. 3264 water bottles for 2/23rd Battn of L.R.	
ERGNIES			↑ S290 do. 2/22nd Battn of L.R.	

Army Form C. 2118.

SANITARY SECTION
60th (LONDON) DIVISION

Sheet No. 5.

WAR DIARY
or
~~INTELLIGENCE SUMMARY~~ Medical
(Erase heading not required.)

Instructions regarding War Diaries and Intelligence Summaries are contained in F.S. Regs., Part II. and the Staff Manual respectively. Title pages will be prepared in manuscript.

Place	Date	Hour	Summary of Events and Information	Remarks and references to Appendices
AILLY-LE-HAUTE-CLOCHER	18/11/16		District Inspections as usual.	
YVRENCOURT			↑ S348 disinfected 800 Blankets & 1200 other articles for 2/20th Battn.	No. 1.
BORENFLOS			do do 600 do & 3000 do 2/18th Battn.	
VILLERS-SOUS-AILLY			↑ S290 do 869 do & 360 do 2/21st Battn.	
VILLERS-SOUS-AILLY	19/11/16		↑ S290 disinfected 1080 Articles for 2/21st Battn.	No. 2.
MOUFFLERS			do do 225 Blankets & 400 other articles for 2/24th Battn.	
			do do 128 other articles for A.S.C.	
GORENFLOS			↑ S348 do 250 Blankets & 500 other articles for 2/18th Battn.	
DIVL. AREA	20/11/16		District Mor. with Brigade fatigue parties concerned to Scavenge Divisional Areas as vacated by troops.	No. 3.
VAUCHELLES-LES-DOMARTS			↑ S290 Disinfected 360 Blankets & 782 other articles for 2/24th Battn.	
			114 do & 496 do A.S.C.	

Army Form C. 2118.

WAR DIARY
~~INTELLIGENCE SUMMARY~~ Medical

(Erase heading not required.)

SANITARY SECTION
56th (LONDON) DIVISION
Sheet No. 6

Instructions regarding War Diaries and Intelligence Summaries are contained in F. S. Regs., Part II. and the Staff Manual respectively. Title pages will be prepared in manuscript.

Place	Date	Hour	Summary of Events and Information	Remarks and references to Appendices
DIV. AREA	21/11/16		Continued scavenging Divisional area in Brigade movements, with fatigue parties from respective details.	
VAUCHELLES-LES-DOMART	22/11/16	9 a.m.	Pte Greenstock with Ford Lorry TS348 left to report to A.D.M.S. 33rd Division at HALLENCOURT.	H.S.
do			586 Blankets 1760 Other Articles for 2/6th Hill Ambce ↑S290 Disinfected " 65 " " 35 do for A.S.C. attd. 6 do	H.S.
AILLY-LE-HAUTE-CLOCHER	22/11/16		Drivers Mahy & Crawford reported with 1st Line Transport as per W.E. Part XII Drivers Grove & Davey do Train Transport	H.S.
AILLY-LE-HAUTE-CLOCHER	23/11/16		Aired Limbers with Stores & Baggage. Surveyed Ailly-le-Haute-Clocher Village & Billets.	H.S.
AILLY-L.H.C.	24/11/16		No. 3022. Cpl C.F. MANGOLD transferred as Sanitary Cpl to D.H.Q. for purposes of Manoeuvres.	
		9-20 a.m.	Proceeded out of AILLY by Motor Lorry with Personnel & Transport & Mules, by route march to LONGPRE arriving a/c	H.S.
LONGPRE		10-15		
		5-15 P.M.	Drivers Hugglett & Garnett with Thunder Lorry Y5374 } Swervived to report to O.C. to Tomlinson & Hickey with Foden Wathill No. S290. } 5th Army. Petrol Coy at AILLY.	
		6-30 P.M.	Entrained Personnel & Mule Transport & left for LONGPRÉ.	

A58-4 Wt. W4973/M687 759,000 8/16 D. D. & L. Ltd. Forms/C.2118/13.

WAR DIARY
— or —
INTELLIGENCE SUMMARY.
(Erase heading not required.)

Army Form C. 2118.

SANITARY SECTION
60th (LONDON) DIVISION

Sheet No. 7

Medical

Place	Date	Hour	Summary of Events and Information	Remarks and references to Appendices
MONTEREAU	25/11/16	4 p.m.	Arrived on train – 50 minute halt.	H.S.T.
MACON	26/11/16	9 a.m.	Arrived on train – 60 minute halt	H.S.T.
PIERRELATTE	26/11/16	6.45 p.m.	Arrived on train – 50 minute halt.	H.S.T.
MARSEILLES	27/11/16	2 A.M.	Arrived at 2.A.M. Detained with transport	H.S.T.
		5 a.m.	Proceeded with Personnel & Transport to LA VALENTINE CAMP.	
MARSEILLES	28/11/16		Unit resting.	H.S.T.
MARSEILLES	29/11/16		Assisting with Sanitary Supervision at LA VALENTINE CAMP.	H.S.T.
MARSEILLES	30/11/16		Packed Transport Limbers & delivered at Berth No. 12. for Embarkation on R.N.T. "MANITOU".	H.S.T.

H. S. Tebbutt
Capt.
O.C. SANITARY SECTION
60th (LONDON) DIVISION

www.ingramcontent.com/pod-product-compliance
Lightning Source LLC
Chambersburg PA
CBHW081449160426
43193CB00013B/2418